Angus Fraser was born in Lancashire in 1965. He made his Middlesex debut in 1984, was awarded his county cap four years later and a benefit in 1997. His England debut came in 1989 in the third Test against Australia at Edgbaston. On his return to the national side after recovery from a career-threatening hip injury he took the Man of the Match award as England beat Australia for the first time in seven years. Although dropped by Illingworth after the 1995–96 tour of South Africa, he was recalled for the 1997–98 tour of the West Indies. He was created an MBE in the 1999 New Year's honours list for his services to cricket. By the start of the 1999 season, he was in England's all-time top ten of wicket takers, with 177 in 46 Tests. In recent years, Angus Fraser has been a regular contributor to the *Sunday Telegraph*.

Paul Newman is the associate sports editor of the *Sunday Telegraph*, having previously worked for the *Daily Mail* and the *Daily Telegraph*. He is the author of *Larger than Life*, with David Smith, and *Ashes Summer*, with Steve Waugh and Nasser Hussain.

my tour diaries

the real story of life on tour with england

ANGUS FRASER

HEADLINE

First published in 1998
by HEADLINE BOOK PUBLISHING

First published in paperback in 1999
by HEADLINE BOOK PUBLISHING

10 9 8 7 6 5 4 3 2 1

ISBN 0 7472 5982 8

Typeset by
Letterpart Limited, Reigate, Surrey

Printed and bound in Great Britain by
Mackays of Chatham PLC, Chatham, Kent

HEADLINE BOOK PUBLISHING
A division of Hodder Headline PLC
338 Euston Road
London NW1 3BH

contents

introduction

Touring is the ultimate. I can't imagine there being a better way of spending three to four months of your life than playing a game you love at the highest level, being paid reasonably well to do it, and spending time with a group of people you have a lot in common with. It's a privilege and a lifestyle I wouldn't swap for anything.

I have been fortunate enough to go on six full senior tours with England and this book is a taste of life on those tours. A seventh, to Australia in 1998-99, ended in disappointment, with the Ashes lost 3-1.

What I have tried to do is provide an insight into the events, both on and off the field, that have occurred 'on the road' with England since my first trip to the West Indies early in 1990. I have picked out the most eventful two Tests, both from an individual and a wider perspective, on each trip and based my account of each tour on a detailed look at them. I have also tried to provide an insight into the characters of the leading figures on those tours, both in the England side and from the opposition; players who have been influential in my career as well as towards English and world cricket. There is also a look at the background to each tour and its aftermath, to offer a more rounded view of the 'history' of the English cricket team abroad over the last decade.

There is, of course, a recurring theme on all of my tours: we have lost the Test series on each occasion, a sobering and disappointing thought. This book seeks to look at why that has happened and offers suggestions as to how things could be improved.

I made my Test debut in 1989 against Australia and at that time, the distinguished journalist Reg Hayter, who has now sadly passed away and who was president at my cricket club, Stanmore, suggested I keep a diary. He told me I would never know when it might come in useful and that it would be nice to look back at events on the cricket field and off it in future years. I followed that advice and have been painstakingly recording my thoughts and feelings after each day's play, at home and abroad, ever since. Those diaries form the basis of my recollections for this project and have allowed me to recall exactly how things were at the time and how famous Tests and infamous incidents occurred.

Indeed, there have been plenty of major milestones in my time. They include the drama of victory at Sabina Park against the mighty West Indies in my first overseas Test and the controversy of Trinidad later in that tour; the complex and sometimes uneasy relationship between Graham Gooch and David Gower that was such a feature of my first tour of Australia; the ignominy of the team being dismissed for 46 in Trinidad in 1994 and the superb fightback that earned victory in the next Test in Barbados; the heartache of being left out of the 1994–95 Ashes trip and the subsequent joy when I returned to the squad as a replacement and experienced victory against all the odds in Adelaide; the sheer determination of Mike Atherton's magnificent match-saving century in Johannesburg and the awful collapse and recriminations of Cape Town in early 1996. They are all here.

A lot of people like to keep their innermost feelings to themselves when they are away from home, but I am quite happy to share the experiences. That was why I agreed to Derek Pringle's request to publish extracts from my diary of the 1994 West Indies tour in the *Independent*. Later, when I toured South Africa, the *Sunday Telegraph* made a similar request and thereby began my relationship with the paper which continues today.

I enjoy travelling. I wasn't a great fan of flying when I first started but the number of flights I've had and the amount of miles I've covered have made me much more relaxed about it now. You could say I've been very lucky with the tours I've been on because I haven't, to date, spent a long time in the sub-continent. All the places I've been to have offered a similar lifestyle to home. That may sound boring, and I know many people travel to see contrasting countries, but I'm working when I'm on tour and have to be in the right frame of mind for work. Perhaps I haven't made a big enough effort to get out and about and see the countries I have toured, but I have always been of the opinion that I could go back as a holidaymaker another time. When I am on tour with England I am there on business and need to use whatever time I get off to relax and recharge the batteries.

I've seen most of the major sights in Australia, which is a fantastic place. It's such a fresh and exciting country and its history does not hold it back. People there go for life without worrying about what they should and shouldn't do. Over here in England, wonderful though it is to have a history, the decision-making process is made much harder by the constraints of tradition. Sydney is my second favourite city in the world after London, and all the other major

3

Australian cities are pretty similar with the exception of Hobart, which has the feel of New Zealand, or Scotland, about it.

I like Australia and the Australian way of doing things. Their sports system works and they use sport to promote the country. I had spent time there playing grade cricket before I toured with England, so the country was pretty much what I expected. As was the West Indies. I've been to nearly all the bigger islands and have enjoyed most of them. Barbados is gorgeous, Antigua and St Lucia are lovely, while St Vincent is perhaps as nice a place as I have ever visited. It is tranquil, untouched West Indies at its best. These contrast with Jamaica, which is big and rough, Guyana, which is more of a third world country, and Trinidad, which is somewhere in between Jamaica and Barbados.

South Africa, though, was a bit of a disappointment. That said, Cape Town is brilliant and, while not quite being in Sydney's class, is right up there with the world's best cities. But the other places were not as impressive as I thought they would be, Johannesburg and Durban being quite intimidating and the other cities and towns were very quiet.

Touring is not all fun, though there is plenty of fun to be had. Being away from home does create pressure and I'm sure many wives and girlfriends wonder what we're up to when we're away. They know we're out mixing with people and it can cause a lot of tension. Things do happen on tour and it's no coincidence that the divorce rate among cricketers is pretty high. When I first went away on tour I enjoyed my independence and the freedom to do what I wanted to do. It's harder now with a family. Denise and I have two children, Alex and Bethan, and you do get lonely at times when you're away. My children brighten up my life and I'm like anybody else, I miss them, but I'm lucky: Denise is an excellent mother and wife, and she is well supported when I'm on tour by both my parents and hers. Many cricketers moan that they don't see their families but if I was to count up the days I spend at home in a year, it would come to more than someone with four weeks' annual leave, I'm sure of that.

The bottom line is that I enjoy what I do, which makes going away that much more acceptable. There are more positives to touring than negatives – as you will see.

england in west indies 1989–90

The background

I came onto the England scene at a time of great uncertainty. Not only were the team on the end of an Ashes drubbing by Australia but the 1989 series was disrupted by the announcement, in the middle of the fourth Test, of a second England 'rebel' tour to South Africa. For a young, impressionable and proud player like me, it was the most graphic of eye-openers.

I played in three of the six Tests in 1989 and would have appeared in the final match at The Oval, too, had I not twisted my knee trying to stop a four with Australia something like 600 for four in a typically one-sided encounter that summer. There had been talk of a rebel tour all year and the matter came to a head during that Old Trafford Test. I remember it distinctly. At that time the England side, somewhat bizarrely, used to change in three different rooms at Old Trafford while the visitors had the Lancashire dressing-room all to themselves, and I was in a little room at the back with John Emburey, Neil Foster and Graham Gooch. Because it was the most private place, I used to sit there watching the cricket on the television when I was not on the field – I have always preferred that, for some reason, to watching 'live' from the balcony – and one by one various England players used to come in to see Embers, who seemed to be at the centre of things, and discuss with him whether they were going to South Africa or not.

It was disappointing, to be honest. I was playing in only my second Test and as far as I was concerned there was great prestige and honour in playing for my country. But here were several senior players who were clearly disillusioned enough to decide to turn their backs on it all to earn a bit more money while they could. It was as though playing for England didn't mean as much to them as it did to me. Some players found making that decision easier than others. I can remember Neil Foster bowling in tears at Old Trafford thinking that this was the last time he would play for England. I don't think it affected me long-term, but it did bring home to me at an early stage why so many England sides are not as competitive or team-oriented as, say, Australia. There was a mercenary attitude in the air during that match at Old Trafford and money seemed to be at the root of the players' actions. That was sad.

That summer also ended with the replacement of David Gower as England captain by Graham Gooch, even though Gower, like Gooch, was one of the senior men who had decided not to go to South Africa. I don't think the possibility of the England captaincy had anything to do with Graham turning down the chance to go on what would have been his second rebel tour – in fact, I'm sure it didn't – but now he had been handed what many considered the poisoned chalice of leading England on tour to the West Indies, the hardest place of all to win at that time, after a convincing and thoroughly demoralising Ashes thrashing by the old enemy. And to cap it all, many of our best players had made themselves unavailable by turning their backs on England and heading off to South Africa. Surely we didn't have a hope in the Caribbean?

Well, that's what everybody thought. But what the situation left us with was a young and mainly inexperienced side, led by the world-class example of Gooch, and that was to work to our advantage. For we almost pulled off one of the great Test upsets of modern times in that series and I was in at the thick of it. It was a fantastic introduction to touring.

The West Indies is a great tour for an England player. Not only is it a beautiful place to visit, the timing is so important for your chances of making an impression out there. Many tours leave you with so little time to prepare at the end of an English season that you are either still fatigued from the domestic campaign or underdone in your preparations. Before you know it, you're on a plane to Australia and you are just not ready either mentally or physically. But with a West Indies tour, starting soon after Christmas, at least you can rest when you need to and then get mind and body focused on the task ahead. By the time our raw England party left for the Caribbean that year, we were ready and unfazed by previous disasters over there because so few of us had suffered at the hands of the West Indies before.

Our first commitment that winter was the Nehru Cup one-day tournament for a month in India towards the end of 1989, which went quite well. The bulk of the West Indies party went there, together with a couple of additional selections like Derek Pringle and Nick Cook, and we acquitted ourselves pretty well. We reached the semi-finals and won three and lost three of our six matches there, defeating Sri Lanka, Pakistan and Australia but losing to the West Indies, India and a Salim Malik-inspired Pakistan in the semi-finals.

But that was only part of our preparations. Because we had so much time before we left for the West Indies, we were in a position to prepare properly and so was born a completely different, fitness-led England training regime, spearheaded by Gooch together with a manager in Micky Stewart who clearly thought along the same lines as the new captain. By the end of our training, which included regional get-togethers, I think we were the best-prepared group of England cricketers ever to leave these shores and I found some of the criticism that Gooch and Stewart received for knocking us into shape more than a little harsh. Some people just didn't seem to think cricketers had to put so much emphasis on physical fitness, but surely the fitter you are the better you are likely to do? It certainly can't do any harm. And what was that famous Gary Player quote about the more he practised the luckier he got?

Gooch was certainly very keen on fitness because it had worked so well for him personally and he brought in a fitness expert called Colin Tomlin – who, tragically, died a couple of years ago – who did a tremendous job with us. He got me as fit as I have ever been and I responded very well to him. We used to train in groups, with the A team who were due to tour Zimbabwe included too, and it was a system that I thought worked very well. Colin used to train athletes in Kent and was quite clearly proud and enthusiastic about representing his country when he was working with us. That rubbed off, I believe, on a lot of people. He encouraged us to puff out our chests at the thought of playing for England, and quite right, too.

It was only when we were putting the finishing touches to our preparations during a week at the national sports centre in Lilleshall that we realised how fit we were. Gooch's philosophy had worked for us. He was a successful player and his attitude was that you never got anything for nothing in this world and that the way to get to the top was to work bloody hard to reach it. He argued that you had to control as many aspects of your game as you could and one thing you certainly could control was your fitness, to make sure you were capable of doing the job day in and day out to the best of your ability.

His successor as skipper, Mike Atherton, is similar in many ways. Neither he nor Graham is what you might call an inspirational captain but both lead by example and command respect for what they have achieved on the field. And they have achieved it their way, with their methods, and it was only natural that they would want the rest of us to follow their example.

Micky was very influential in all this in 1989–90. He strengthened Gooch's resolve because he was a similar character. Micky had been successful working with Mike Gatting in Australia in 1986–87 – the Grand Slam tour – but had not really been on the same wavelength as David Gower when he captained the side. Now he was much happier.

I enjoyed working with Micky. He was the closest I've ever known in cricket to a football manager, and that extended to being very thorough in his approach and totally in control of things. It really was a new beginning for England. So many senior men had gone – people like Gatting, Emburey, Broad, Dilley, Foster, Barnett, French and Jarvis – and we were all so new to the scene that we were given absolutely no chance. The West Indies, of course, were the strongest side in the world at that time and were virtually invincible at home. So you could see the point of the doubters.

But the more we trained and worked together as a unit, the more confidence we gained that we could do well out there. People who had been on previous West Indies tours, it seemed to me, had almost talked themselves out of the series before they got there. I remember Phil Edmonds telling me that on a previous tour the batsmen thought the only way to get runs in the West Indies was to try to smash it around before the inevitable throat ball came along to get you. It seemed almost defeatist.

Our policy, one clearly defined by Gooch and Stewart before we left, was to wear the West Indies down when we were bowling and to guard our wickets obsessively, irrespective of the scoring rate, when we were batting. The West Indies tails are always up when they are taking wickets, but we thought that if we could frustrate them, even if it meant scoring only 50 or 60 runs a session, their heads would drop and they would start going on the defensive, which could only be to our advantage.

Only Gooch and Allan Lamb had played a large amount of Test cricket before. There were a couple of other older hands in Eddie Hemmings and Wayne Larkins, but neither had that much experience at the top. We were all in the same inexperienced boat and consequently we all got on extremely well. The biggest feeling as the tour approached was one of excitement. It was all so new – and it was nearly all so victorious.

The build-up

Sometimes we'd tell ourselves in the build-up to the first Test in Jamaica that we would do well, but in the back of my mind I wondered if we were kidding ourselves. Obviously it would have made no sense to go out there with a defeatist attitude because then it would have been a case of 'Why the bloody hell are we bothering?' But as far as I can remember, deep down I really did think we had a chance.

We knew we were underdogs but, speaking for myself, I have never gone into any game expecting to do badly, and I think the others were in the same frame of mind.

Before we got there all we heard about was their four quick bowlers and how terrifying it was going to be. They were going to stick it up us and break our arms, stuff like that. In fact, when I was first picked, Desmond Haynes, then the West Indies vice-captain and a colleague of mine at Middlesex, grabbed me by the hand and started looking at my left arm. I asked him what he was doing and he said: 'It looks as if it could be broken.' It was half in jest but he was trying to intimidate me, too.

But from the moment we arrived in Barbados to the first Test in Jamaica, we barely faced a quick bowler. There were some reasonable bowlers around in the warm-up matches but none of their main men. It was clearly a deliberate policy to stop us facing their Test attack, but I think it worked against them because by the time of the first Test, even though we had hardly played scintillating cricket, all the batsmen had got runs and were feeling quite good. It didn't matter to them who those runs came off, they just knew they had all got hundreds or eighties and all felt quite consistent going into the first Test.

Our first stop was Barbados, the perfect introduction to touring. We practised hard, sure, but it was all so new to so many of us that we enjoyed ourselves, too, perhaps going out a bit more than we should have done. We went bodysurfing most days, jet skiing quite a lot and hired mini-mokes so we could get around the island. Actually, when we went to get our licences for the mini-mokes we encountered a real jobsworth of a policeman who insisted we didn't have the right paperwork with us. Until, that is, he realised we were England cricketers and then it suddenly didn't matter and off we went.

One night, a few of us went to Ricky Ellcock's mum's house for a meal. Ricky had joined Middlesex from Worcestershire at the start of 1989 and had quickly made an impression with his extreme pace and control, so much so that he was included in the tour party and was now back in Barbados, where he was born and grew up, with England. His mum laid on a great meal for five or six of us and we then moved on to a little rum shop Ricky knew. We had a couple there before an interesting return cab journey, during which the cabbie offered to get us anything we wanted while we were on the island, ranging from drugs to laying on women for us! We politely declined and told him we were just there for the cricket!

Ricky, of course, had been the centre of attention when we first arrived on the island. Everybody wanted to meet the four fast bowlers of West Indian origin who were 'returning' to fight fire with fire, as the saying at the time went. So Ricky, Devon Malcolm, Gladstone Small and Phil DeFreitas were all lining up for photos at the introductory press conference and giving interviews, while myself and David Capel, the other members of our pace attack, quietly slipped into the background.

Barbados is a terrific place and I was determined to make the most of the whole experience. We were staying at a good hotel and could afford to eat at decent restaurants. It's funny looking back at my diary now, reliving the whole thing and chuckling at some of the entries. For instance, I wrote early on that 'I have found out how expensive things are over here, so have told Denise [then my girlfriend and now my wife] that she can only come out for the Barbados

Test and not Antigua too as we originally planned.' Needless to say, this didn't go down too well.

The net facilities were good in Bridgetown. A lot of local bowlers came along, all of them pretty quick, and the temptation from our point of view was to look at them and think, 'Bloody hell, they're only club bowlers but they look better than we do.' You soon realise, however, that they're not. It was just this image we had that if they were big, black fast bowlers, they were automatically as good as Sylvester Clarke or Wayne Daniel. The thing is, bowling quickly is not enough at professional level and we were soon reassured that these guys were not actually superior to the England cricket team, when they joined in a couple of practice games and didn't have either the control or the ability to do as much with the ball as we did.

One eye-opener was that the pitches were not as quick as we thought they would be. In fact, they were pretty slow and flat. The outfields, too, were very different. On most English grounds the run-ups are so smooth and carpet-like, but here it was something of a culture shock to see the conditions in which we had to operate. We just had to adapt and get on with it because you can't go to the West Indies expecting all the things you'd get at Lord's. You do get bad footholds, holes in your run-up and bad bounces in the field – no wonder a lot of West Indians field in boxes – but you can't worry about it.

The saddest aspect of our build-up was Ricky having to go home. He had bowled at a genuinely quick pace for Middlesex the previous summer and had moved the ball away from the right-hander, which meant he had a lot going for him. Ricky was an awkward customer. He had Devon's pace but was smaller and skiddier and for such a nice man he was a nasty piece of work with a ball in his hand. Ricky never minded shaking up batsmen.

But as soon as we arrived in the West Indies, his back started playing him up. Since then, I have got to know Ricky really well because he had a recurrence of the problem some time afterwards and it coincided with my serious hip injury, so we spent a lot of time together rehabilitating at the doctor's and with the physio. His back problems eventually forced him to retire from the game, which was very sad, but he's recovered from that magnificently, using what insurance money he got to fund a new career as a pilot. He is now working for Virgin, flying to and from America mainly, and has done very well for himself.

God knows what I would have done if my body hadn't come right after my hip problem. Life's easy when things go well but when it doesn't, it toughens you up and makes you more determined because you realise what you're missing. You do get closer to people too, when things go wrong. My close friendship with Mike Atherton dates back to when we were both selected for the tour of New Zealand and the World Cup in 1992 but couldn't go because of injury. When you share that experience and recover together, it creates a certain bond between you.

In 1990, Ricky was a big part of our tour strategy. We were always going to play four fast bowlers to try to give the West Indies a taste of their own medicine and he would certainly have come into the Test frame. His departure was a big blow to us because he was very popular with the team. He knew quite early on that his back wasn't going to get any better. The crunch came when we were in St Lucia and they told him he had to bowl flat out. When he couldn't, he returned to the dressing-room in tears because he knew his tour was over.

It was difficult to know what to say. We left him alone at first and then tried to get him as involved as we could. We said goodbye to Ricky at a barbecue in St Lucia when both he and I said a few words. I wondered at the time whether bowling on the hard surfaces of Lilleshall had buggered up his back, but he clearly had a weakness there. So he had to go home without ever playing a single game for England and, meanwhile, we welcomed a young, shy Chris Lewis to our number.

Chris came from Middlesex and had played a couple of games for our second team before going up to Leicestershire, but I didn't really know him at the time – he was quiet and a bit of an enigma even then. He came out and was thrown straight into a one-day international when Phil DeFreitas failed a late fitness test on his knee. It was Chris's 22nd birthday and he took a catch off my bowling in the deep, making it look very easy (he also dropped one!) before opening his own account by recording Desmond Haynes as his first international victim – not a bad one to get.

Both of the opening one-dayers in Trinidad were rain-ruined but we did pretty well in them and team spirit was high. There were endless functions to attend, of course, because there is a British high commission on each island. Some were very tedious and to liven things up, Alec Stewart and Keith Medlycott used to indulge in this embarrassing comedy routine at functions in which they would pretend to be each other. There were also endless flights to catch and one of them showed early on just how close we had already become as a team. We discovered, while travelling between St Kitts and St Lucia, that Graham Gooch's seat had been double-booked and they were trying

17

to tell him he would have to catch a later flight. We were having none of this and said that if our captain couldn't get on the plane then none of us would – a case of all for one and one for all. Eventually, they relented and threw out some other poor sod from his seat so that Goochie could be with us. It was the sort of togetherness that, unfortunately, I haven't always experienced on tour.

There was a lot of anticipation as the first Test approached. We had lost to the Windward Islands in St Lucia – to a left-arm spinner who apparently spent his summers playing for Wycombe House second or third teams – but it can be harder to motivate yourself for those warm-up games than for, say, a Middlesex game. Basically, England warm-up games are there for you to get in shape for the Tests. Yes, it's nice to win but it is not the be-all and end-all, so we were not over-concerned about our defeat against a spin-based attack (once again, the top bowlers had been kept from us).

Still no one gave us any chance, and that was made clear to us shortly after I was chosen as one of our four pace bowlers for the Test at Sabina Park. On these occasions you get asked to pose for all sorts of pictures and I thought nothing of being asked to stand alongside the other three members of our attack – Devon, Gladstone and David Capel. It was only after we had won the first Test that I discovered the *Mirror* had published this picture under the headline 'Pop Guns' next to one of the West Indies attack with the headline 'Top Guns'. When we found out about that, it was a question of waiting until I bumped into the people who had written the article and saying, 'Well done, you got that right, didn't you – now p*** off!'

First Test, Sabina Park, Kingston, Jamaica; 24 February–1 March 1990

Day one

My first Test abroad was a huge game for me. It started on my dad's birthday, so I received a nice call from my parents on the morning of the match and then it was a question of getting ready for the action. The wicket looked flat and totally devoid of grass. It was perhaps not as shiny as the one we found four years later, but it was a sort of mosaic, with loads of little cracks in it which were to play a big part in the game as it progressed. Later on, some of them started to disintegrate round the edges, which meant the ball would keep low or do things.

The crowd were immediately noticeable, so different from home and great to play in front of. They were never quiet and polite, like so many English cricket crowds, but really got involved in the game and generated excitement around the ground. Every boundary seemed to be greeted with an explosion of noise and the spectators would stand up and scream and shout their approval or displeasure. Kingston itself was an intimidating place – we were warned not to go out of our hotel alone – and it was a bit like that in the ground, unlike the other West Indian islands.

This was the day when the Gooch 'huddle' was born. A lot of West Indian grounds are quite compact, with the dressing-rooms next to each other and very little glass separating them. You can almost hear what's going on next door, so as soon as the bell went for the start of play we used to go out on the field and have a little chat, with Graham basically reminding us what we had to do on the field and to keep our discipline at all times. Hence the huddle.

Not that it did us much good at the start of this match. We made a poor start and it was almost a case of 'here we go' until we got a breakthrough that changed the course of the match and in all probability the series. Gordon Greenidge and Desmond Haynes, at that stage the best opening partnership in the world, had proceeded comfortably to 62 without loss just before lunch, during which time Devon had misfielded horribly on the boundary near the scoreboard, letting a ball through his legs off Gladstone's bowling.

At that time, Devon was as raw as they come as a cricketer, even though he was playing for England. He was a hostile bowler but had not really worked on his fielding or batting at any time in his career. Micky would spend hours with him doing extra fielding – Devon is a natural athlete and as strong a man as you'll ever meet, so there really shouldn't have been any reason why his fielding was so bad. We had some hilarious fielding sessions with him. The ball would go up and people would shout 'Devon, right hand, right hand' and sure enough he slowly improved.

So when the ball went down to him at fine leg, soon after his spectacular misfield, and bobbled, I thought, 'Oh God, he's going to let it through his legs again.' The ball bounced, hit Devon on the knee and landed a yard in front of him. Greenidge saw this and thought he'd take him on, understandably, but what he didn't know is that Devon has one of the strongest throws you'll ever see – he can throw 100 yards off his knees. And on this occasion, Devon picked it up and let go a throw like a shot out of a gun, right over the stumps, where Jack Russell had the easy task of running Greenidge out. It lifted everyone.

We hadn't bowled that badly up to this point but the

ball hadn't been beating the bat and it looked as though we were in for a long, hard day. With some of the batting they had to come, the match could easily have gone away from us, so to get one of those two out was just what we needed before lunch. We went into the break on a bit of a high and came out afterwards competing, bowling with discipline; so much so that we worked our way through their batting with our 'bore them to death' policy. Goochie had again emphasised to us that we should wear them down and not give them any balls to hit, and this was when Geoff Boycott, who was part of the first Sky TV commentary team to broadcast live ball-by-ball coverage to England throughout a winter tour, started to say that we were bowling down 'the corridor of uncertainty'. That was exactly right. We knew they were a side who liked hitting boundaries and that if we cut out the four-balls, then maybe we could frustrate them into getting their shot selection wrong.

We all managed to do this and had them 140 for five at tea, with Gladstone getting rid of Haynes, David Capel dismissing Richie Richardson and Carlisle Best – now there was an interesting character. He used to commentate on the game when he was batting, saying things like, 'The bowler's running in and Best has hit that beautifully for four' – and Devon claiming the prized scalp of Vivian Richards.

We thought we had got Viv out a couple of times before Devon had him LBW for 21. Gladstone also thought he had him LBW and I thought I'd had him caught behind. But, wherever you play, captains often seem to get the benefit of decisions – they, after all, decide umpires' futures – and, thankfully, the great man wasn't around for too long to spoil our day. This turned out to be the only time I played against Viv in Test cricket, and I'm very pleased I can say that. When I was a kid, whenever I was asked about my heroes, I always used to say first, Ian Botham, because of 1981, and then, always, Viv Richards.

Thinking of Viv conjured up images of him putting his foot down the wicket and whipping the ball over midwicket with his jumbo bat, and he was the one you always tried to imitate as a kid. I'd played against him, of course, in county cricket and I bowled him in a Sunday League match towards the end of his career with Somerset – he had hit me back over my head for six and then got bowled two balls later. So Viv was a big reason why I wanted to play cricket in the first place. He was a genuine superstar, with his swagger and the way he played his cricket, and they don't come along too often.

I only really faced him when he was past his best, but he scored a double century against Middlesex for Glamorgan at Cardiff and, in a masochistic sort of way, it was a real pleasure to be on the end of it. It was the same when I played against Martin Crowe in a Test against New Zealand at Lord's and he scored a fantastic century. When you look back at your career, you want to be able to say that you played against the best at their best, and you want to appreciate how good these people were – it's never the same when people tell you about these things. Viv's 200 that day was magnificent. He didn't slog, he got stuck in, collected his runs and hit the bad balls for four. It was great to witness how good he was and to have something I could remember about the man.

Viv normally asserted himself as soon as he arrived at the wicket, coming out to play three or four big shots straight away at the start of his innings just to take away any initiative the bowler might have, and the ground would erupt when he walked in. He would never let you dictate to him and was always a daunting prospect to bowl to. I had seen him destroy attacks over the years and when he walked out that day at Sabina Park, I thought: 'Well, I'm in that position now. What's he going to do to me?' Thankfully, it wasn't too bad.

Viv was never one to say much on the field. His body language did all the talking and, in any case, his record spoke for itself. He did have something to say later on at Sabina when, with the wicket deteriorating, I came out to bat in our first innings wearing my bowling boots, to see if I could scuff it up a bit. After I'd walked up and down the wicket a couple of times, Viv tumbled what I was up to and said to me, 'Hey, what do you think you're doing?' I soon stopped. You didn't argue with Viv.

He was under a lot of pressure in this series. After we won in Jamaica, he made a statement saying that the West Indies would recover because of the African spirit in the side, which didn't go down well in Guyana and Trinidad where there is a large Asian population. In fact, Viv got booed to the wicket in Guyana before missing Trinidad through illness, which was quite a contrast to his usual reception.

On this first day in Jamaica, the roof came off when he arrived, as usual with a cap rather than a helmet, to try to rescue his side. I remembered Ricky Ellcock telling us from his experience in West Indian domestic cricket that the best place to bowl to Viv when he first came in was well wide of the off stump, because he would always go for it and do something silly. But I thought: 'I can't do that. The captain will go spare if he leaves four wide balls outside the off stump. You've got to make him play.' But any worries we had about what Viv might do to us were ended when Devon struck, and there was a very excited atmosphere in our dressing-room at tea.

Yet I was still to get a wicket. My diary reminds me now that I was feeling a bit tired during the break but as all their batting bar Carl Hooper had gone, the plan was for me to carry on after tea for two or three overs to see if I could break through. My first ball did the trick – Hooper trying to pull me and being caught at mid-on. With my next ball I bowled Malcolm Marshall, then I got Ian Bishop caught at slip and finished with five for 28 off 20 overs. It was just one of those little spells that comes along every now and then when it suddenly goes bang and you get four or five wickets in as many overs. You can't explain it, it's just the way the game goes sometimes. Most days you walk off the field thinking you're the unluckiest bowler in the world and cursing your luck, but then these little spells come along to restore your faith in humanity and this was one of them. It was brilliant. The ball reverse-swung for me – a fairly new phenomenon at this stage – and it all went right.

To walk off the field having taken my first five-wicket haul for England – admittedly it was the tail – and with the West Indies all out for 164 in a match everybody expected us to lose gave me a real buzz. When things go for you like that, there's nothing in the world anybody could say to you that would wipe the smile off your face.

We were euphoric, but also apprehensive. It was like we'd got them out but this would now be what the West Indies was all about. Now we would witness at first hand what we'd seen on TV – four hostile, quick bowlers peppering you. Everyone in our party without exception watched that last little session when we began our innings. No one was distracted and no one could take their eyes off the play. It's worse watching than bowling because there's so little you can do and on this occasion we were all a bag of nerves, standing on the balcony with the crowd all around us.

The West Indies threw everything at us that night. We started superbly before Gooch got strangled down the leg side for 18, a good catch by Jeff Dujon off Patrick Patterson, and then Alec Stewart came in and hit his first ball in Test cricket for four, an early indication of the way he plays. Alec made 13 before he was out but we ended the first day on 80 for two, a tremendous position to be in. English supporters came up to me after play to say I had made their trip, which was really nice, but I wrote in my diary that 'I must make sure I'm not a one-match wonder. Remember Patterson's T-shirt [all the West Indies bowlers were wearing them at this time and it was the first time I'd seen the motto]: "Form is temporary, class is permanent." '

Day two
When I was young, the thought of facing quick bowling terrified me. Then, the more you experience it, the more you become accustomed to the pace and it doesn't seem quite so bad. You start to think about these things logically. I'm not express pace but I still run out of puff, and it doesn't take a genius to work out that it must be the same for these guys. You also realise that if you make them work for your wickets they can go on the defensive and go into their shell, waiting for something to happen rather than making it happen. This day was the epitome of that.

Allan Lamb and Robin Smith played excellently in a partnership that won us the match. So jealously did they guard their wickets that at one stage, the West Indies were reduced to bowling two spinners, Richards and Hooper, in tandem. We had simply worn them down. The quick bowlers had thrown everything at us, getting Ned Larkins out for a good 46 to a poor decision, but they couldn't make any further breakthroughs. Lamb and Smith didn't smack the ball around but they got the runs we needed.

Lamby is a character who doesn't let anything worry him. He's always full of beans, always full of life and organising something. There was never a dull moment on tour with Allan Lamb. He's good company and good fun to be with and he was always lining up a trip for the boys or an evening with one of his many friends who just happened to be on the island. He knows everyone and is always busy, scheming and wheeling and dealing. You do need that sort of person on tour.

It was not all play, though. Lamb was a very hard-working and conscientious cricketer who put a lot of determination into making himself the magnificent batsman he became, particularly against pace bowling. He was such a good cutter and puller, like so many small men, and showed enormous guts in confronting every situation that came his way.

The challenge was always there against the West Indies, which was perhaps one reason why he always did so well against them. He often didn't do quite so well against lesser opposition, maybe because they didn't push him like the best did. When life was a bit easier he didn't seem to get the best out of himself and maybe let his concentration waver a bit, hence his failure to turn many of his centuries into really big ones. It was almost as if he had done what he needed to do in reaching three figures and was then going to enjoy himself.

On this day Allan and Robin emphasised the closeness of their friendship, something that had started before and had built up by the time we got to the West Indies. They were almost like Siamese twins on tour, always together and always out. 'Judgey' was almost like Lamb's apprentice, his gofer, but they got on so well and that was noticeable on the pitch. They just didn't want to let each other down.

Robin was eventually brilliantly caught by Best off Bishop for 57 to end a stand of 172 for the fourth wicket, but Lamb recorded his 10th Test century, five of them having come against the West Indies. He actually reached the landmark twice, hitting a great pull shot and accepting the congratulations of us and the crowd before the scoreboard clicked back to 99. Then he played another great pull shot and both his hands went up in the air. What an achievement!

After he went for 132, the rest of our innings was fairly quiet but Nasser Hussain, another debutant like Stewart, also got off the mark in Test cricket with a four, with his second ball, and went on to have an identical innings to Alec – they both scored 13 off the same number of balls with three fours and a single each. Uncanny really, particularly as they are both still going in Test cricket and have both had spells as Mike Atherton's vice-captain, before Stewart succeeded him. We finished the day on 342 for eight with me not out on one. I wrote in my diary: 'I'm not out and I look good!'

Day three

We increased our overnight lead to exactly 200 before we were dismissed for 364, with me unbeaten on two and still looking good; a formidable lead in the circumstances and, really, a position of strength beyond our wildest dreams before the match. I remember thinking, when they started their second innings, that the next passage of play could win us the match, but they had a pretty decent little session with useful contributions from Greenidge, Haynes and Richardson before, with Best still there but Hooper gone, the moment of truth arrived.

Everything went quiet on the field, but not in the stands, when IVA Richards walked in with his side 112 for four, still 88 behind. We all knew this was the big moment and you could feel the tension in the air – Viv's presence can change any game in an hour. He played pretty well in reaching 37, showing us that he knew how much depended on him by playing patiently and with care, until the moment when we knew we could win the game. Devon Malcolm came on and Viv went bang, bang, bang and then out. Devon had gone for a few but had then beaten Richards with sheer pace to york him and claim the biggest wicket for the second time in the match. It was a great moment.

From then on, everything went smoothly. Gladstone Small bowled really well to dismiss Best, the top scorer with 64, and at the close they were just 29 ahead with only two wickets standing. Victory was within our grasp and everybody was jubilant. That night we had to go to a Cable and Wireless function, but we turned up a bit late because we'd all been enjoying our situation, sitting there in the dressing-room with a beer and soaking the whole thing in. After our official duty was out of the way, the evening continued – and two of our players, who shall remain nameless, told their girlfriends, who were out with them at the time, that they were needed for more official duties and had to go out with us rather than them! They just wanted to be with the team. The fun went on in the team room and I had a bit more to drink than I should have, mainly because of two magic words – Rest Day!

I had a game of tennis on the morning after to try to sweat out the night before and then had lunch around the pool. Suddenly, though, there were, literally, giant clouds on our horizon. The weather had taken a turn for the worse and it was now raining heavily. This worried us enormously. We couldn't believe that rain, in the West Indies of all places, might spoil it for us after all our hard work. We just wanted to get on with the game and had an early night, desperate for the rain to stop and almost chomping at the bit to get the job done.

Day four

My diary reminds me that I called this the most frustrating and annoying day of my career to date. I see no reason to argue with that now. As soon as we woke up, a glance through the window told us the awful truth. Just to confirm what we already knew, we were told not to bother going down to the ground as there was no immediate prospect of play. Sabina Park was under water. All of us just sat around in our rooms, waiting for news. It was still overcast and there was rain in the air. Lunch was a very solemn affair. After eating, we all went down to the ground to have a look at the situation ourselves and to put a bit of pressure on the groundstaff to dry things up as quickly as humanly possible.

It was still drizzling, and very wet at the George Headley Stand end. Apart from that, the only really wet patches seemed to be on the bowlers' run-ups, which led me, in my depressed state, to write in my diary that 'it smells of foul play'. The groundstaff seemed to be doing very little to clear the outfield and some of them even said they didn't want to see the West Indies' proud record at Kingston ruined so they weren't going to rush to get things dry!

It was obvious there would be no play all day, so I went to the Sky control room with a few others to watch highlights of the first three days. It was all very exciting having Sky on this tour. It added to the sense of what we were doing being important to the people back home, because they could see every ball of an overseas tour, a real luxury then for the cricket enthusiast.

Eventually, play was called off for the day and we went back to the hotel to play a bit of tennis before going for a run, during which it absolutely poured down again. It was awful. We wanted to win so much and all we could do was sit around helplessly, not knowing what to do with ourselves. We just shook our heads and waited for the weather to improve.

Day five

All through the night it was a case of lying in bed, half asleep, wondering if each noise I heard was more rain or a tree rustling. Having done so much to set up victory, this was like a nightmare. Often as a cricketer you pray for rain, but not this time. The moment of truth came when I woke up and headed for the curtains. They revealed blue skies and an incredible sense of relief. But how wet was the ground? Would we start on time?

Everyone was keen to get back to business, but when we got to the ground we discovered Micky Stewart had been there since 7am, almost supervising the groundstaff and making sure everything was done properly! Patches of the run-ups were still wet, but they were drying out quickly and the umpires decided that play would start on time. By now we were faced with the amazing sight of virtually only Englishmen coming into the ground and hardly any West Indians at all. It was a shame the ground was to be almost deserted for our big moment.

When play started, Courtney Walsh decided to play a few shots and quickly got bowled by Gladstone Small, and then, in the next over, Malcolm Marshall and Patrick Patterson got involved in a mix-up which resulted in a run-out. It couldn't have gone better for us. Devon and Gladstone finished with four wickets each and were given a great reception by the people on the ground as they walked off, with us needing 41 runs to win and most of the day to get them.

Gooch and Larkins made a great start, which they needed to do because the West Indies bowled very well, clearly not wanting to go down quietly. When we were in sight of the winning post, Goochie fell to a brilliant catch by Greenidge in the leg gully, which was a great shame. Everyone had wanted the captain to be there at the moment of victory. He had quickly earned our respect as a team because of the way he conducted himself and went about his work. We all wanted him to hit the winning runs, but it was not to be.

By this time we were desperate to get the game over before lunch because we were worried the weather might turn again during the 40-minute break. We need not have worried. Ned 'kitchen-sinked' a four then got a single off a misfield to start the party. Allan Lamb got the Man of the Match award and there was champagne everywhere in the dressing-room. The best part of our celebrations was the journey back in the coach because we were on our own as a team for the first time and that meant something after what we had achieved.

When we got back to the team room at the hotel, we discovered the press had donated a case or two of champagne and there was also plenty of Tetley's to enjoy, too. It meant so much to everyone, particularly the senior players who had been on the receiving end of so many hammerings from the West Indies and had never beaten them before. Somebody then told us that it had been 16 years since England last beat them in a Test.

Our young side had been given no chance of succeeding; we were expected to be lambs to the slaughter but we had been the totally dominant team. We received so many messages of congratulations, including a telex from the then prime minister Margaret Thatcher. It was quite clear to us immediately that it meant a lot to people. The celebrations went on long into the night and we had deserved it. The whole tour had been set up.

The interim

If I needed any reminder how quickly cricket could kick you in the teeth, it came just a couple of days later when we played a one-day international at Sabina Park. The West Indies needed two runs off the last ball and I was the bowler. Ian Bishop hit me for four and I stayed standing, hands on hips, in the middle as the crowd flooded on before

Graham Gooch consoled me and led me off. I wouldn't say it spoiled Jamaica, but it was a pain – Geoff Boycott said to me afterwards, 'Well, at the end of the day you weren't good enough. You had to put the ball in the right place and you didn't do it.' Thanks a lot, Geoffrey!

Our adventure soon took us to Guyana, which had a reputation for being the least developed country of those we were to visit and a climate in which it was always raining. It didn't disappoint! It was maybe the only place on tour where you felt you had to be careful with the food you ate, a place where Jack Russell would try to survive for two weeks on cold beans and corned beef. Jack once had a whole case of beans sent over there at the start of a tour, which he planned to make last for the whole trip, but this thing was the size of a cricket 'coffin' and no one wanted to carry it. So it stayed in Antigua for the whole tour.

It just rained for a week while we were in Georgetown. The Bourda Ground was under water all the time and there were fish on the outfield. The second Test never even began. I was sharing a room with Wayne Larkins and we were woken up each morning by rain coming through the ceiling and dropping on our faces – and this in the best hotel in Guyana. We ended up playing an extra one-dayer in Georgetown when the rain finally stopped, just to keep everybody there happy, but we lost that one, too. In the end we were grateful to move on to Trinidad for the third Test, particularly Nasser, who, it turned out, had broken his wrist playing tennis against Phil DeFreitas to pass away the time in Georgetown, an injury that wasn't diagnosed properly at first but one that was to keep him out of the bulk of the 1990 English season.

On each tour, the powers that be make sure we're never

in Trinidad while the carnival is on. It's a lively island at the quietest of times but during the carnival it's absolutely crazy and they don't let us go anywhere near it! Our arrival, soon after the carnival, cheered us bowlers up because we thought the Queen's Park Oval would be the most helpful wicket for us to bowl on, with grass on it and a more tropical atmosphere than Jamaica. That proved to be pretty much the case.

Before the Test, we played Trinidad in Point-à-Pierre and had our first glimpse of a young Brian Lara. I wasn't playing in the game as I was resting but we all travelled to the ground, smack in the middle of an oil refinery, every day with Micky to support those playing. Then we would go to a local club ground to have a net among ourselves. Micky, in fact, broke his finger during one of these sessions trying to keep wicket to me!

Lara, indeed, got a hundred but we won the game. Even then he was being talked about as a special player, even though he had yet to make his Test debut, and I remember him being a small lad who played similarly to the way he does now, all flowing cuts and drives.

This match was also notable for Robin Smith ending on 99 not out in the second innings, left stranded after Devon Malcolm, the last man, had arrived at the crease promising Robin that he would play for him to make sure he got his hundred. Devon took an enormous slog at his first ball and got an inside edge for four; then he blocked two before having another great slog and getting bowled ... Well, Devon couldn't stop apologising to Judgey, telling him he didn't know what had come over him, but his batting was very much in character. Usually, if he survives his first ball, the show begins!

The rain in Guyana had not done us any harm. It had just increased the pressure on the West Indies. They now had to win two out of the three Tests that remained to win the series, which is what everybody expected them to do and that was a difficult proposition even for a side like them. Results-wise, the tour had not gone brilliantly for us, but we had won the game that mattered and were now in very high spirits. The West Indies, meanwhile, had problems. Patterson was dropped but, most significantly, neither Viv Richards nor Malcolm Marshall was fit. Desmond Haynes was to lead a side which suddenly had a big question mark over it. You could tell they were feeling the pressure because they were not used to losing in the West Indies and usually they just steamrollered teams. It was a lovely position for us to be in and we were thoroughly enjoying it.

Third Test, Queen's Park Oval, Port-of-Spain, Trinidad; 23–28 March 1990

Day one

And we enjoyed the first day of the third Test, too. I was a bit nervous going into the match, which was unusual for me but all of a sudden we were in a position to create history, so that increased the pressure we all felt. I was still determined, also, not to be a one-match wonder.

My diary tells me that this was 'a very good day for us but it could have been better'. That sums it up. We'd certainly have settled for the position we closed on at the start of the day; it was just that it could have been so much better.

Trinidad is an unbelievably hot place. The heat, of course, can affect people in different ways but Trinidad is very humid, which makes it hard work for me. I sweated buckets on this day. Each time someone slapped me on the back it just made a wet sound where I was soaked through. I seemed to spend all day with a bead of sweat hanging off my nose and just had to take on as much fluid as possible. Looking back now, I see that I wrote in my diary that my hip hurt throughout the day – now that's something I had completely forgotten but is hugely significant when I think of what I went through with my hip in subsequent years.

Pain and fatigue, however, were the last things on my mind when we had the West Indies at 29 for five after winning the toss and putting them in to bat. It was unreal. At that stage we thought we could bowl them out for 50 or 60, but Gus Logie played superbly until I had him strangled at gully cutting for 98. He had come into the side for Viv and he led a real recovery act, mainly in partnership with Ian Bishop, to get them up to 199. From where they were it was riches indeed, but still not a good total – that's what we had to remind ourselves.

I didn't bowl that well for one reason or another, which was a shame because it was a good wicket to bowl on, as we'd hoped it would be. Yet I finished with three for 41 off 13.1 overs so, as it was an off-day, that was OK. Everybody was knackered because of the heat when we came off. Devon was again the main destroyer with four wickets, but everybody had contributed to another excellent performance. It was as if we were dreaming.

Then Gooch and Larkins saw us through to 43 without loss before bad light ended play early, and I discovered that Ned had had a £100 bet with Martin Johnson, then the cricket correspondent of the *Independent* and now with the *Daily Telegraph*, that he would score a century the next day. I could see why Ned was so confident. Things were really going our way.

We had suddenly got into a spell where we could do nothing wrong and at the end of the first day we had them by the knackers. It was a situation England had been in on far too many occasions, but you could see in their cricket that the West Indies were missing their usual spark.

Day two

We batted very slowly again, working on the principle of not losing too many wickets to try to knock the edge out of their game. It was overcast for much of the day and the ball continued to move around. In a way we were quite lucky, because the ball beat the bat quite often but we didn't lose many wickets. Ned got a maiden Test 50 but, unfortunately, lost his bet with Johnson, being dismissed for 54 by Curtly Ambrose, who was back in business after missing the first

Test and the perfect replacement for Marshall. Alec Stewart played better than his score of nine would suggest, but, most of all, Goochie showed enormous concentration to finish the day on 83 not out. Bad light had stopped play early again but we had fulfilled our objective of 'winning' another day's play and were on our way again. We had lost just two wickets in the day and had scored 150 runs. With three days left, we'd have settled for that again.

Day three

It rained just before the scheduled start of play and we lost 100 minutes. Then, when we did start, the wicket had greened up under the covers and was more difficult than ever. We started 20 minutes before lunch, which was a bad time for us, and lost Graham in the first over of the day for 84 to a very excitable West Indies side. Cricketers are very superstitious people and usually you do not move from your spot in the dressing-room when things are going well. But I had just left the pavilion for the first time during our innings to do a lap with Alec Stewart when Gooch was out, and was still walking around the ground when we quickly lost Lamb, Smith and Rob Bailey, who had come into the side for the injured Nasser.

For the first time in the game, or the series, West Indies looked on top, but we battled it out until tea with David Capel doing well. Soon after the break it was my turn to face the music and I found myself facing Bishop, who I felt was bound to let me have a couple of bouncers to begin with because I'd hit him when he batted during their innings. He did let me have some short stuff but I played it OK and began to really enjoy myself in the middle. Like most things, it was never as bad as I feared it would be out there and I was having great fun until, on 11 and after me and David had put on 40 for the ninth wicket, I tried to play my first shot and was caught at slip off Ambrose. The light wasn't very good but we got up to a lead of 89 with Capel being the last to go, hooking, for 40. Our lead was good but not as good as it might have been and we missed the chance to get among them before the close when Devon, the silly sod, bounced Greenidge, prompting the umpires to take us off for bad light. That night we had another Cable and Wireless do and went on to a party at a friend of Allan Lamb's because, you've guessed it, the next day was a rest day!

Generally, I miss rest days now they are such a rarity in Test cricket. We could have done without it in Jamaica because we wanted to finish the job, but usually five days' Test cricket is very hard work and you need a break. I can only remember having one rest day in a home Test – at Old Trafford when the Sunday coincided with the Wimbledon tennis final – but generally they're a good thing to take your mind off the cricket and gear yourself up for the final couple of days. The game should be a test of stamina and fitness, but not to the extent that you're on your last legs.

Day four

A day that turned out to be another good one for us, but not before we endured a frustrating morning session which turned out to be the first in the series so far in which we hadn't taken a wicket. I was, initially, struggling to get my rhythm but that all changed in the space of two overs. First I got Gordon Greenidge out LBW to what even I would admit was not a good decision – *Wisden* reports that Greenidge was 'visibly disgusted with the decision' – and then Devon got three wickets in the next over, six balls which changed the game completely.

Haynes, Best and Dujon all went in that inspired Devon over and all four wickets that fell in the afternoon session had come in two dramatic overs. The West Indies, at 100 for four, were in big trouble again. When another five wickets went down after tea, we were looking at another win, incredibly. Devon was again the main man, but Gladstone and I chipped in and they closed on 234 for nine, just 145 ahead. I felt so strong I could have bowled all day and I know the others felt the same. Graham told us we could be part of history the next day and that we should behave accordingly that night – though I don't think anyone would have stayed out late, with us in that position – and I wrote in my diary: 'Who'd have thought we would be in this position and have the West Indies by the short and curlies when we arrived in January?' Devon, mean-while, had clearly unsettled the West Indies because he was quicker than any of their bowlers and that shook a few of them up. We had both made our debuts against Australia the previous summer, so this was only his third Test yet he was looking world class, having taken nine wickets so far in the match (he would make it ten the next day).

Yet Devon has not always reached those heights since. He's a very quiet, shy man and at this stage I didn't know him too well. Obviously, you could see how physically strong he was, but he has never been the most confident person and I think even Graham Gooch struggled with him at times. He would tell him to bowl short to someone but Devon would keep on pitching it up and vice-versa. It seemed to be a confidence thing rather than Devon being awkward, but by the end of the series Graham was almost asking Devon to do the opposite of what he actually wanted him to do.

If I had to be slightly critical, which I don't like to be because nobody could ever accuse Devon of not giving 100 per cent, I would have to say that he does drift a bit. In his 'coffin' Devon has got a card with the words 'stop dreaming' on it and a mirror below, so he is obviously aware of it. Nobody is perfect, but this might explain why he has been inconsistent at times. When he gets it right he's a fantastic bowler, as he has shown on several occasions, but I think he would agree that for England he hasn't got it right quite often enough throughout his career. I think sometimes when he's played for England he has tried to bowl too quickly. When he does this his action changes, causing him to push the ball in to the batsman rather than move it away as he does day in and day out for Derbyshire. These flaws in Devon's action have drawn the attention of several England coaches over the years who have each tried to help him. Devon, to be honest, could have been more responsive to their efforts, but throughout a career you get as much bad advice as good – it is up to you to work out which is which. At the end of the day it is your career and you are wrong if you go around blaming other people for your failings. It is you who lets go of the ball.

When he does get it right, as we have seen on so many occasions, particularly in this match, Devon is a high-quality bowler capable of bowling as quickly as anyone in the world. It is just a bit frustrating that this has not happened as often as everybody would have liked. People have said that he and I have been the best English opening attack for some years because we complement each other so well: there's Devon with his hostility and me with my nagging accuracy at the other end. Yes, he can be a bit expensive, but with me at the other end any captain would be happy to tolerate that.

Has Devon been handled properly? Well, he certainly wasn't in South Africa in 1995–96 but you could say the same about a lot of bowlers in the last ten years. Devon has been in and out of the side, but again, so too have a lot of other bowlers. It can, however, affect your confidence and someone like Devon does need to be nurtured and treated with tender loving care. He needs to feel as though he's a big part of the team and have the freedom to go out onto the field and throw everything at the opposition. He's been on most senior tours throughout his career and has been given a fair crack of the whip, but because his bowling has been inconsistent at times, so too has his selection. I don't think he'll be an unfulfilled talent if he never plays again for England. I suppose he will leave the game as something of an enigma, but anyone who can take ten wickets in a match against the West Indies on their own patch, or nine in an innings against South Africa at The Oval in 1994, can look back with pride at some of the things he has achieved. He's always been fully committed to his country and his team, and it could all come down to the fact that he's too nice in many ways.

He's a gentle, meek man who just wants to get on with his life and maybe he needed to be a bit nastier to thrive in the highest company. For instance, when we went back to the West Indies in 1994 he was given a dreadful going-over by Courtney Walsh when he batted, but he didn't really hit back when he had the ball because he's not like that. Devon won't give up hope of playing for England again, I know that. He could easily come back into the reckoning. We

(*Above*) A key moment in the Sabina Park Test of February 1990: Gordon
Greenidge is run out by Devon Malcolm. (*Below*) Suddenly the wickets began to
tumble for me, and I finished up with five for 28. (*Patrick Eagar*)

Another appeal is turned down – Viv Richards, like so many home captains over the years, was always hard to get a decision against. (*Patrick Eagar*)

Devon Malcolm was one of our chief destroyers in the second innings at Jamaica. (*Angus Fraser*)

Allan Lamb took over as captain for the last two Tests of the series, and was always at his best against the pace of the West Indian attack. (*Patrick Eagar*)

Dean Jones was one of my victims on the way to my then best Test figures of six for 82 at Melbourne in December 1990. (*Patrick Eagar*)

David Gower tries to cheer me up during the third Test at Sydney, as the hip injury that was to take me out of action for so long began to take hold. (*Ben Radford/Allsport*)

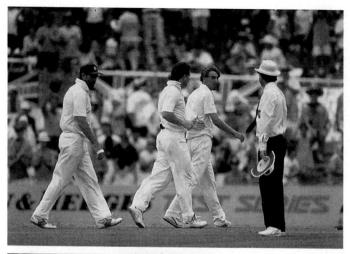

Phil Tufnell and the umpire argue at Sydney – it was not the happiest tour for him. (*Ben Radford/Allsport*)

Allan Lamb, on the other hand, thoroughly enjoyed touring and was able to chill out whenever the chance arose. (*Angus Fraser*)

shall see what happens; it's down to him to show how much desire or motivation he has left in him.

Day five

After Devon had taken the last wicket we were left with 151 for victory and virtually all day to get them. But what was to follow was not the cruise to victory that we had hoped for and expected but a day's play that remains among the most controversial that I have ever been involved in.

I wrote at the time: 'This is the worst day of my career. Certainly the most frustrating, as bad as in Kingston when it rained. For them to get away with a draw after all our hard work is a total downer and hard to take. If we'd won this match, the very least we could have gained was a drawn series and something to be proud of, but the way the West Indies played was a disgrace.'

It all went smoothly to begin with. Twenty-five came from our first six overs before Larkins fell to Ezra Moseley, who looked as quick and dangerous as any of their bowlers after coming in for Patterson. But what really hurt us was when Moseley hit Graham Gooch on the hand, a blow that forced him to retire hurt. With him went the series.

We did not know that at the time, of course. When it happened we were all told the captain's hand was only bruised and that he was planning to go back in if we lost quick wickets. He really is a gutsy sod. He must have known it was broken but he didn't let on in case it affected our morale. But still we were cruising home until the rain came during the afternoon. After Sabina, we just couldn't believe this was happening again.

When we eventually got back out there, 78 were

required from 30 overs with plenty of wickets in hand, but such were the West Indies' delaying tactics that only 17 were bowled in barely fit conditions and we had to settle for the most frustrating of draws.

For a while it even looked as if we might lose the game. We lost wickets at regular times and there were those people who said afterwards that we should have chased the target right to the end, but in those conditions, against that sort of bowling, we were always going to struggle to get home. Besides, those who criticised us for accepting the draw didn't have to sit there, as I did, padded up and gazing into the gloom fearing I would have to go out and bat!

We were 31 runs short of our target with five wickets left, one of which belonged to the injured captain, when we called the chase off. The rain had come suddenly and turned our leisurely afternoon into a frantic chase, with a couple of batsmen perishing aggressively.

Yet the major talking point afterwards was the West Indies' tactics, overseen by their stand-in captain Haynes, which led me to make that emotional diary entry, even though I followed it up with this: 'There was a bit of sledging out there but it was blown out of all proportion by the press and there was no ill feeling afterwards between the sides. We have got on with them very well, even though there are a few who don't make much effort to say much when you go into their dressing-room at the end of a day's play.'

Truth is, everybody pushes rules to the limit if they can and most cricketers get away with as much as they can. But I personally – and I'm sure the England team of that time and now – would never take the piss out of a situation and never push the rules to the point where it became embarrassing. We'll slow a game down if it suits us, but only by one or two overs, not by the amount that the West Indies did that evening. Nobody likes losing, but their actions showed how desperate those guys were not to lose. I can't really say how wet it was in the outfield but their bowlers were making a hell of a lot out of it. The amount of times Bishop, for instance, pulled up in his run-up was daft, and it was ridiculous how the umpires let them get away with it. I don't think it would happen now we have neutral umpires, that's for sure. The overseas umpire would step in and make them get on with it.

This game was galling. Their players seemed to have decided that they would accept fines if it meant they could get out of the Test with a draw, because it's the winning and losing of series that people are remembered for. We all play the game hard and nobody wants to lose, but it's a question of how far you push it.

Being in the dressing-room was desperate. All this rain was really testing our resolve. So many times in cricket when you are in a winning position, the weather interferes and it affects the way you play. When we finally came off, Jack Russell wanted to carry on but David Capel wasn't so sure. I could see his point. There was only me, Gladstone and Devon to come and to have lost that match from the position we were in would have been a disaster.

There was a lot of anger aimed at Desmond Haynes but most of it came from our frustration. We were angry that we weren't going to win but we were also relieved that we hadn't lost, so it went full-circle in one afternoon. Dessie was under a lot of pressure. It was his first Test in charge and he's a very passionate, demonstrative character. He'll always react to a situation, never walk away from it and he can be aggressive, too. I'm surprised he didn't do better as the Sussex coach – mind you, he didn't have much to work with – because he's very disciplined and a pleasure to play with; but not against. On a cricket field he is ruthless.

I remember going into the dressing-room in Trinidad to have a drink with Dessie after that last day's play, so there couldn't have been too much bad feeling. He basically tried to emphasise to us the pressure he was under and he was saying things like: 'You don't know what it's like playing over here.' It was not an apology for his tactics, more an explanation. Apparently, when he was playing for Barbados, people would ring him up at home after a day's play telling him what he'd done wrong on the field and in the end, you react to that sort of pressure.

The England team are under tremendous pressure but with us it comes from the press, whereas out there it comes from the people. In the Caribbean, if you are a member of the West Indies side that loses a Test, never mind a series, you keep a low profile because the locals don't make life pleasant for you, and I'm sure this pressure got to Desmond Haynes in the third Test.

He was a magnificent player, make no mistake about that. He did really well for Middlesex and was highly regarded by the younger players, who used to sit around and listen to his every word. It's significant, for instance, how many of them switched to an open batting stance like his – just look at Mark Ramprakash. They took to Desmond instantly and benefited tremendously through working with him. He made time for the younger players and cared for them, not just because it was an obligation but because he wanted to.

That level of commitment is not something you see in all overseas players. Desmond Haynes wanted to play for Middlesex and he contributed a great deal to the club. He helped me, too, making me a little more aggressive on the field and harder to beat. He emphasised little things like always make sure your first ball is an effort ball because good batsmen will be looking for the loosener and will hit it for four, and, surprisingly, don't be shy of bowling a few more short balls.

Haynes played some brilliant innings for us and was very intense about his cricket. He is a proud man who doesn't accept failure and I clearly remember him putting his fist through a door at Headingley because he was so depressed about a run of poor form. Myself and Nasser Hussain clashed with him during the Bridgetown Test later on that tour after Rob Bailey was given out down the leg side, controversially. We were livid and had words with Haynes as we walked off the field because we knew Rob wasn't out and tensions were very high, but with Dessie it's never a long-term thing and it's all quickly forgotten.

I've had a few run-ins with him over the years. I suppose it's a bit like the Robert Croft and Mark Ilott incident in the NatWest semi-final in 1997: you often clash with people you know the best. For instance, on the last tour of the West Indies we had an exchange of words after my hand had been broken on the field, and later that day he sent a bottle of Listermint to our dressing-room so that I could wash my mouth out! He has, of course, had some more serious arguments with a couple of Australians, but from what I gather there has been a racial element in that, so you could understand him getting upset. Race would never, ever come into an England v West Indies match.

Generally with Dessie it's a spur of the moment thing and then it's forgotten, and I would rather someone care than not show any emotion. I happen to think an exchange of words is not really a big deal, particularly when you compare the aggression in cricket to what goes on in other sports. The odd fracas when people are playing with intensity is not the end of the world.

The aftermath

Trinidad was, however, the end of my tour. Soon after, as England were preparing for the fourth Test with a warm-up match against Barbados, I was asked to bowl to David Gower, who had been put on stand-by for the fourth Test, in the nets but I suffered a rib injury and put myself out of the last two Tests. I kept on having fitness tests and like to think I play through most things, but I couldn't play through an intercostal injury. I could have coped with a one-dayer, perhaps, but not bowling 40 overs in a Test match.

That was a blow to our side but not nearly as big as the absence of Graham Gooch with his broken hand. Soon after Trinidad, Ezra Moseley went on to break the thumb of David Smith, who had flown in as Gooch's replacement; and with Nasser playing on with his broken wrist, we were beginning to struggle a bit.

Even so, we still very nearly drew the Barbados Test. There was the Rob Bailey incident – which proved that Viv Richards was under just as much pressure then as Haynes was in Trinidad – but we held on until Ambrose, who seemed to be saving his wickets up for when it most counted, got our last wicket later than the designated close-of-play time. It was a sickener.

By then the West Indies were getting stronger and stronger and we had to go straight to Antigua for the final Test. They just blew us away with an intensity which proved how well we had done to peg them back for so long up until that point. Their bowling was at its fiercest in Antigua, so much so that they shook Robin Smith and Rob Bailey up. They won the match and had got out of jail.

There was an empty feeling when we got back home; a real case of what might have been. Yes, we achieved a great deal on that 1990 tour of the Caribbean and came back with our heads held high, but the bottom line was that we came back with nothing. To see it all disappear was heart-breaking, but our pride remained very much intact.

England to the West Indies 1989–90

First Test
Sabina Park, Kingston, Jamaica, 24, 25, 26, 28 February, 1 March
West Indies 164 (A.R.C.Fraser 5 for 28) and 240 (C.A.Best 64)
England 364 (A.J.Lamb 132, R.A.Smith 57, C.A.Walsh 5 for 68) and 41 for 1
Result: England won by 9 wickets.

Second Test
Bourda, Georgetown, Guyana, 9, 10, 11, 13, 14 March
Result: Match abandoned.

Third Test
Queen's Park Oval, Port-of-Spain, Trinidad, 23, 24, 25, 27, 28 March
West Indies 199 (A.L.Logie 98) and 239 (D.E.Malcolm 6 for 77)
England 288 (G.A.Gooch 84, W.Larkins 54) and 120 for 5
Result: Match drawn.

Fourth Test
Kensington Oval, Bridgetown, Barbados, 5, 6, 7, 8, 10 April
West Indies 446 (C.A.Best 164, I.V.A.Richards 70) and 267 for 8 dec
(D.L.Haynes 109)
England 358 (A.J.Lamb 119, R.A.Smith 62) and 191 (R.C.Russell 55,
C.E.L.Ambrose 8 for 45)
Result: West Indies won by 164 runs.

Fifth Test
Recreation Ground, St John's, Antigua, 12, 14, 15, 16 April
England 260 (I.R.Bishop 5 for 84) and 154
West Indies 446 (D.L.Haynes 167, C.G.Greenidge 149)
Result: West Indies won by an innings and 32 runs.

Angus Fraser's tour (1st and 3rd Tests):
Batting: 2 innings, 1 not out, high score 11, runs 13, average 13.00.
Bowling: 71.1 overs, 18 maidens, 161 runs, 11 wickets, average 14.63, best
5–28.

england in australia 1990–91

The background

Whenever I have toured the West Indies it has always seemed a new beginning, from my first tour in 1990 to the comeback from serious injury in 1994 and, most recently, my selection for the 1998 tour after being written off by many as a Test bowler. Australia, however, has been different.

My two trips there have both come when I expected to be picked – even though the second was as a replacement – and have arrived almost straight after a demanding domestic season. Consequently, I have not quite enjoyed Australia so much.

Australia is still special, because it's a fabulous place. You get looked after extremely well, the hotels are magnificent and there is no shortage of things to do or places to go. The practice facilities are first-class and all in all, you get spoilt rotten. But, maybe because I was expected to do well, rather than experiencing the elation of a trip when I haven't been a certain selection, the tours there have not been as much fun for me.

I missed the first half of the 1990 season with the rib complaint I sustained in the West Indies, which meant I did not play in any of the three Tests against New Zealand. I did, however, come back for the three-Test series against India, which proved to be a highly entertaining and momentous little series. I actually got eight wickets in the first match against them at Lord's but was overshadowed by a certain Graham Gooch, who scored the small matter of 333, and also by Mohammad Azharuddin, who produced one of the best centuries I have seen later in the game. Why do I always seem to record my best performances when other people hog the limelight?

The Indian series produced some good, hard cricket and I bowled well against a strong batting line-up on wickets which were very flat because of the new regulations that instantly weighed the game much more in favour of the batsmen. Now pitches had to be straw-coloured and the seams on the balls had been reduced. For someone like me who is essentially a seam bowler, this was bad news and I felt it was bound to make me a less effective bowler because it was taking away two of my biggest weapons. The game was going to be much harder from now on.

A 1–0 series win put us all in good heart for the winter ahead – again a departure from the normal mood when we tour the West Indies, which recently has been in the wake of an Ashes defeat leaving us with a nothing-to-lose type attitude that has worked in our favour. Another big change was the inclusion of David Gower in the party after his match-saving performance against the Indians in the final match at The Oval.

The other notable development of 1990 came quite early in the season when I was still recovering from my rib injury. A businessman called PJ Mir approached the majority of the England side proposing a short tour of Toronto and New York for the end of the season, before we left for Australia. Around £4,000 each for a week's work was on offer, so of course most of the players, including captain Graham Gooch, were pretty keen on that, and as we were not contractually obliged to turn it down, we all signed up. The Test and County Cricket Board, however, were not happy. We only had three weeks between the end of the season and our departure for Australia and we were going to spend one of them playing exhibition stuff in North America. But the TCCB could do nothing about it because we were free to do what we liked before joining up for the Ashes tour.

As far as I was concerned, when I signed up, this was the only work I was guaranteed for the winter and I didn't feel as if I had a commitment to the TCCB. So off we went on this little 'rebel' tour, enjoyed a nice earner and didn't pick up any injuries, so it was fine and much fun was had by all. New York has to be the most intimidating but exciting city I have been to. It doesn't sleep. It's an amazing place, but you feel aware of lots of potential danger. Indeed, one night after an official dinner we got back to the hotel at about 1am. Our intention was to go and have a look around Times Square, as you do. Jeffrey Dujon, the West Indian wicketkeeper, an opponent of ours on this trip and a frequent visitor to New York, physically stopped us from going, saying that we wouldn't come back with everything we went out with. This coming from someone who lived in Kingston, Jamaica, which is certainly not one of the friendliest places. Jeffrey worried a few of us, so we retired to bed and all got home safely.

Soon after that, the TCCB decided to put some players under contract for the following winter, including me, to stop us doing it again. Then they caught a bit of a cold on that when some of us were injured and couldn't tour but they had to pay us anyway. Now they have it written into our contracts that we can't undertake trips like these before departure, so unfortunately it won't be happening again.

We all felt pretty good before leaving for Australia. Our preparations were a bit rushed, but we did squeeze in a visit to Lilleshall and tried to get the balance right between resting after a hard season and working hard to get ready for the tour. I don't think, though, we were quite as united as when we left for the West Indies. We had had much more time then to build team spirit and get our minds tuned to the task.

It was apparent even then that the Aussies had a mental hold on us. We knew they were going to be a hard bunch and, to me, Test cricket had suddenly become a serious business. The romance of the West Indies just didn't seem there. Yet there was an enjoyable build-up to departure. I went to Buckingham Palace for the first time as part of the Middlesex team who had won the championship that summer and collected the Lord's Taverners Trophy from the Duke of Edinburgh. Then, on the eve of our leaving, Graham Gooch was done for *This is Your Life* on TV, which meant us all springing a surprise on him when Michael Aspel appeared with his red book. I'll never forget Allan Lamb having a few drinks before delivering his lines and, when a worried producer asked if he was OK, saying, 'Don't you worry about me, china. I've got my bit ready. Just crack on!'

The build-up

There's always a special excitement on the day you leave to go on tour. Getting on a plane as an England team with your blazers on, travelling business class on British Airways and getting well looked after, being in the bubble of the Jumbo Jet and having a good laugh with just the team present. I just wish I could afford to do it this way when I travel with my family!

As usual, Allan Lamb disappeared into first class to nick some wine for us because he wasn't happy with the business-class selection and we settled down to what seemed a very quick 24-hour journey before arriving in Perth, a smashing place but perhaps not one of my favourite cities because it lacks real character. I like a bit of dirt about a place and a sort of lived-in look. Of course, I had already had experience of Sydney, where I had spent an extremely beneficial winter playing for Western Suburbs, and I suppose I was comparing Perth to there. I remember being extremely impressed with the Australian set-up as soon as I arrived in Sydney in 1988–89, and even then I thought we should be looking to bring a lot of their methods into our game. Cricket is serious stuff out there, especially at club level. It really does leave our league cricket in the shade. Grade cricket is very hard and competitive and there is no room for the social cricketer. With the structure beneath so strong, it is no wonder they now beat us so regularly.

One of the highlights of my first Ashes tour came very early on in the piece. Allan Lamb and Robin Smith were good friends with Dennis Lillee and, on our second night in Australia, they took me to his house for a meal. I have to say that it was one of the greatest nights of my life. Imagine being invited to spend an evening with one of the best bowlers of all time, and a man who has always been a hero and an inspiration to you. The three of them were laughing and joking all night, while I just quietly sat there in awe of Dennis.

Just to be in his company and listen to him talking about his cricket was brilliant. Lillee and Richard Hadlee have always been the bowlers I've looked to learn from, watching them live or on TV to see what they do. There was a real skill to their bowling, accurate as well as attacking, and they clearly used to think about what they were doing. I saw Dennis's famous signed picture of the Queen – which he asked her for during a tour of England and which now hangs proudly in his front room – and generally had the time of my life.

We began our build-up in Perth, where the surfaces had a reputation for being quick and bouncy. They didn't disappoint. In fact, the nets were as good a surface as you could hope to bowl on for bounce and consistency, which suited both bowlers and batsmen. Our preparations were going well – until a freak injury which did much to undermine our Ashes chances before we had even started.

When Graham Gooch injured his finger trying to collect a caught-and-bowled chance offered by Robin Smith in an early practice match between ourselves, it seemed a routine enough blow. True, it was a bad cut, but Graham went to hospital and had some fly stitches put in it. We didn't think it would be long before he was back playing. But it nearly became a very serious problem.

The wound turned septic and became so bad that the poison almost spread to his palm, a development which before the advances of medical science could easily have resulted in Graham losing his hand. And for us, it was an enormous blow to our preparations for the first Test. The captain had been an inspirational figure, his batting had improved with responsibility and he was the one person you were sure would lead you to a big score when you sat and watched him in an England match. Now we had to get on without him.

We started off with a win against an invitation side at Lilac Hill, near Perth, which is the Australian equivalent of Arundel and a nice way to start a tour. Then we lost a match against a Western Australia side at the WACA which offered me my first experience of cricket under lights. It was thoroughly enjoyable, a real thrill and it is an area of the game that I have enjoyed ever since. I clearly remember Jack Russell standing a yard outside the 30-yard circle keeping to Chris Lewis and realising just how bouncy Perth was. Bowling there then, and in the first-class game against Western Australia, was new to me and unlike anything I'd ever experienced. The extra bounce meant that my usual length was now too short and people like Graeme Wood and Ken MacLeay were pulling me regularly until I sorted it out.

From there we moved on to Adelaide and the worst flight I have ever experienced. It was a short flight up country to Port Pirie and for 45 minutes it was like being on a rollercoaster. The warning signs were there before we got on board when Phil Tufnell, who is a bad flyer at the best of times, asked the pilot which way we were going. When the pilot said 'over there' and pointed to a mass of dark clouds where a thunderstorm already seemed in progress, Tuffers turned white and grabbed his St Christopher before getting on.

Everybody panicked once the flight started – and what made us worse was the pilot asking for someone at the back of this tiny plane to move down the front and sit with him to improve the balance. I began to worry, thinking, 'Is 15 stone really going to make that much difference?' Robin

Smith was invited up there while our heads were hitting the roof, we were being bumped so much. Laurie Brown, the physio, was swigging at a bottle of Drambuie to calm his nerves; Tuffers was sitting with his head buried in the back of the seat in front and sweat dripping off his hands with the fright of it all. The stewardess was petrified.

Then, at our lowest point, everybody just started laughing together at the same time. It was as if we couldn't be any more scared and we suddenly realised there was nothing we could do and broke out into nervous laughter. Whether or not we survived was out of our hands. When we got off, hugely relieved, Robin told us the pilot wasn't concerned about the turbulence at all and was just sitting there calmly asking him about the tour. Robin said he felt like saying, 'Bugger the tour, you just keep your hands on the wheel.' I wish we had been that confident.

To cap it all, we lost against South Australia and it was evident now that we were struggling to get our act together. Gooch was still in hospital, unable to play – he was going to miss the first Test – and hugely disappointed that he couldn't go to see an Eric Clapton concert Eric had given us tickets for. Still, Eric gave him a signed compact disc.

Another pleasant distraction in all this was a trip to Geoff Merrill's vineyard near Adelaide. Before this trip, a bottle of Liebfraumilch was the limit of my wine-drinking, but I soon realised how great Aussie wine was and began a love affair with wine that carries on today. At the time, a few of us talked about setting up a little business to import their stuff here, because it wasn't that big in England then and you could clearly see the potential. How I wish I'd done that – I'd have made an absolute killing.

Our trip then took us to Tasmania, where we always

seem to play immediately before the first Test. I didn't realise just how far it was from Brisbane and the difference in climate. It can be bloody cold in Tasmania and we went from a game where we had to wear two jumpers to the tropical heat and humidity of Brisbane. That takes quite a bit of adjustment and is clearly not the ideal itinerary for the start of a series.

At Brisbane we met up with Graeme Hick, who was playing for Queensland and practised with us a couple of times because he was due to qualify for England the following summer. He actually joined us at a local school where we had our nets and the standard of the surfaces was top class. It's so important to have good practice facilities and it's something that is often lacking in England. Can you imagine what would happen if we asked the Australians to go and practise at a school or club ground over here? They would soon be back complaining that someone might get killed, whereas over there, there are plenty of places where you can get good practice. The school nets we were at were better than Lord's.

We got in a good position in the first Test at Brisbane without cashing in, a scenario that was to become depressingly familiar in the coming months, even years. We had a lead of 42 on the first innings in a low-scoring match but then collapsed badly in the second dig, allowing them to win comfortably by 10 wickets. It knocked the stuffing out of us.

In the absence of Gooch, Allan Lamb was our stand-in captain and he was involved in an incident that people remember the Brisbane Test for more than the result. At the close of the second day, with our leader on 10 not out, he was invited by Kerry Packer to a casino for the evening.

I think Tony Greig was there, too. Now Packer is a very wealthy man who gambles fortunes, and when he wins fortunes he tends to give a large casino chip to the people who are with him. Of course, Lamby stayed there later than he should, hoping Kerry would turn around his luck and, unfortunately for him, got spotted leaving the casino fairly late. I'm pretty sure he hadn't been drinking and Allan Lamb, in any case, is a character who doesn't need much sleep, but he left himself open to accusations that he wasn't being professional by being there and it became worse in the morning when he was out to a poor shot during the first over of the day. He didn't even get his chip from Kerry Packer, either, because Packer hadn't had any luck at the tables.

The players weren't aware of any incident until after the match, so it didn't have any effect on us; but it didn't do much for our reputation as we went one down in the series. So often on tours, you feel you have to be doing the right thing almost to keep the press happy. I had also brought some bad luck on myself by telling everyone, when we played Western Australia, that I couldn't see what all the fuss was about in facing Terry Alderman and that I could keep him out. So what happens? He gets me out twice in the Test for nought and one. I could also feel my hip hurting in this match, a sign of the turmoil to come for me.

The next three weeks saw us playing a variety of one-day games which, again, we didn't do well in. We just weren't playing well as a side and a lot of soul-searching was going on. We were getting a lot of bad press and, quite honestly, we deserved it. And our injury problems had even stretched to Micky Stewart, who had to go to hospital for tests when he lost feeling in his legs. I'm sure it must have been the pressure. The one glimmer of hope on the horizon was that our captain was back in time for the second Test at Melbourne, a match that was to become a momentous one for me both in terms of achievement and sacrifice.

We all went to the fancy-dress shop in Melbourne on Christmas Eve to get kitted up for the traditional party. At this time, new tourists had to put on a show for everybody – which doesn't seem to happen now – and there was also a social committee who laid on events and team get-togethers. It was the committee who gave us all a letter to guide us in our choice of fancy dress, and I ended up going as a jolly green giant. Denise was a gangster's moll and there were many other weird and wonderful sights including Mike Atherton as Lucifer, Allan Lamb as a bunny girl, John Morris as Bishop Tutu, Alec Stewart as Hitler and Devon Malcolm as Dracula. There was also the sight of David Gower as a First World War pilot, which, in view of what was to happen to him later on the trip, was somewhat apt.

We practised on Christmas Day, which wasn't very popular with our wives and girlfriends. Micky Stewart certainly wasn't flavour of the month as we ate our turkey. Lindsey Lamb, Allan's wife, complained that it wasn't fair on the children who were there not to have their fathers with them when they were opening the presents, and Robin Smith and Lamby did their warm-ups with Christmas hats on. It wasn't a strenuous session, but it got us going.

We went back to the hotel, where the families had been enjoying a champagne reception, to dress up for the fancy dress and then had lunch wearing it before the new tourists – Atherton, Tufnell, Martin Bicknell and Morris – did their show. 'A Question of Sport'. Tuffers was brilliant, impersonating Graham Gooch wrapped up in bandages doing press-ups all the time. The day then ended with everyone drifting off to do their own thing and we had a quiet night before the Test.

Before the tour started, two days really stood out for me on the fixture list: the first day of the Melbourne Test (Boxing Day) and the one-day international at Sydney on New Year's Day. I knew they'd be watched by big crowds and I was really looking forward to them. My hip was giving me concern but not enough to keep me out of the match. I was getting pain and discomfort but I didn't know what it was and thought it would go away with time. You tend to play through niggles and I just presumed this was another example of that, an injury a fast bowler has to play through.

They were building a new stand at the MCG so there was just a board at one end of the ground, stopping us from seeing this vast stadium in all its glory. But it was still a magnificent place and there were 50–60,000 in there on Boxing Day, so it lived up to its advance billing.

Second Test, Melbourne Cricket Ground; 26–30 December 1990

Day one

We had a good Boxing Day. We finished at 239 for four, after losing a couple of early wickets, and Gower played really well in reaching 73 not out by the close. Mike Atherton was out for a duck but Wayne Larkins chipped in with 64. This did much to calm me down because before the start, I was more nervous than I can ever remember. I just couldn't watch the game. I'm a bad watcher when we're batting at the best of times, but this time I just sat in a corner of the dressing-room, which is down in the depths of the stand, playing with a video game, trying to keep my mind off what was happening in the middle. Unfortunately, the one thing you can't keep out is the noise of the crowd. You keep thinking every cheer is a wicket.

When your team is having a good day, you try not to move from where you are in case it brings bad luck, so basically I just stayed put all day. My work was ahead of me.

Day two

The day started off fine with David reaching his hundred before becoming one of six wickets for Bruce Reid. It wasn't a typical David Gower century by any means, because he was workmanlike rather than stylish and wasn't in the best of form going into the match. But he knuckled down and did well.

Still, we didn't get the score we should have done. I slogged 24 and we ended up being bowled out for 352 when 400 would have been about par. Reid had bowled well at Brisbane and now he was in tremendous form, proving a real handful for us and showing just what a good bowler he was when fit. Reid, of course, had an injury-blighted career and had the sort of spindly frame that couldn't have helped him carry the load of a pace bowler, but I felt really sorry he wasn't able to fulfil his potential, because he clearly had ability. Bruce had a lazy sort of action and was a whippy left-arm-over bowler who hit the bat harder than it looked. He had a lot of things going for him but being built like a rake clearly wasn't one of them. It's sad when injuries stop someone achieving what they could have done, but perhaps it wasn't particularly sad for England that Bruce never toured here, because he always did well against us. Melbourne, though, proved to be his greatest moment.

We bowled badly (me, in particular) when it was Australia's turn to bat and let them get up to 109 for one by the close. There were, however, mitigating factors, not least the weather. That afternoon was incredible. The winds in Melbourne normally come in off the coast, not inland, but every now and then they get what are known as 'norther-lies' which come in straight off the desert. It's a strong wind which feels just like a hairdryer being blown in your face and we had this to contend with all afternoon. I didn't seem to be sweating much but when I went to wipe my brow with my hand, about an inch of salt came off my face. It was the most knackering, cramping session of play I've ever known. It was just ridiculously hot and the wind made all the litter from around the ground swirl all over the place, making it horrible to play cricket in.

It's not an excuse because we played poorly, but we lost the initiative that afternoon. I was shattered at the close. Sometimes if I've had a bad day I like to sit quietly in a corner of the dressing-room after play, thinking things through. A lot of players can't get out of the ground quick enough, but I just like to absorb myself in my thoughts and by the time I left the dressing-room that night, everyone else had gone back to the hotel. So I started to walk back – it was only about a mile away – and a supporter stopped and offered me a lift. He also picked up Geoff Boycott, who was there working in the media, and the journey proved to be a great help to me. It was, in fact, one of the few times Boycs has been really useful!

He said to me: 'You bowled badly, but you're a good bowler and you just have to be patient and wait for it to happen. It's a flat wicket, so just remember what you're good at, keep your discipline and wear them down.' It was, I suppose, fairly obvious stuff but it was constructive and I listened. Geoff was telling me things I already knew and things I would have been telling myself before the next day's play, but it was nice for someone to reiterate it for me. It sort of backs up your conviction.

Day three

Geoff's words must have helped, because I made reference to them in my diary at the end of the next day. All I could think about that morning was what he had said and, also, I kept thinking back to a game we played against Glamorgan the previous summer. I'd bowled badly on that occasion, but I'd sat down in the dressing-room thinking about it and come in the next day and got six for 35. Now the same thing happened again.

The weather had improved, which was a help, and the wind had dropped, but I bowled well, got into a good rhythm and was extremely economical. My first spell saw only five runs come off nine overs and that really set the tone for the rest of the day. We got the initiative back a bit and as the day went on I kept on picking up wickets, to the point where I returned figures of six for 82 in 39 overs, which was fantastic.

It was still hot and I was shattered again at the end of it, but it was lovely. There was still a big crowd, something like 25–30,000, and I got a standing ovation when I walked off at the end of the Australian innings. It was a different type of performance and thrill to when I got wickets in Jamaica a year earlier, because this had taken a lot of effort and the wickets had taken their time in coming. But it had gone like a dream. Every now and then one of their batsmen would nick one and Jack Russell would take the catch (Jack took six catches in the innings) and I was a very satisfied man.

Now ever since then, people have questioned my work-load that day and wondered whether it was the day when I finally asked too much of my body, resulting in the serious hip injury that almost finished my career. But I've said it before and I'll say it again: if you're bowling well and bowling better than your team-mates, then, naturally, you're going to bowl more overs than them. It's unavoidable. I'd bowled 13 overs the previous day and 26 on this one, which is a lot, but I wanted to carry on. If you're taking wickets, the match situation dictates that you should carry on. You just hope your body's strong enough to take it.

Yes, my hip injury was probably the result of doing too much over a period of time, but I want to bowl, I want to take wickets and my attitude has always been that if someone else takes a wicket, that's one I could have got. So you always want to be in the thick of it all; it's horrible to be on the edge of the action. I want to be bowling at crucial times. People have subsequently criticised Gooch for over-bowling me and maybe he did, maybe he could have been a bit stronger with me; but I wanted to carry on all day and I could understand the captain wanting to continue with me, because I was doing the job for him.

I can't remember any one instance of him asking me if I was OK to continue, but I'm sure he did and I would have said 'I'll have another over' and then another one. I've always been like that, it's part of my nature. If I'd been a person who said 'I'm only going to bowl six overs each spell and that's it' then I wouldn't have achieved as much in the game. So it has been worthwhile.

The most important thing is, although I've had my injuries, I've been fit enough to carry that large workload over the years, so I've been happy to do it. Sometimes I've struggled more than others and I remember the Test in Guyana in 1994 where I was just crap. I bowled three overs and I started cramping in both legs, and I said to the captain, 'Athers, I just can't bowl any more.' He has never let me forget that. Most other times, fortunately, I've been able to cope with the workload put in front of me.

There is not a seamer in the country who has bowled more overs than me since I first started playing Test cricket. I know I don't look like an athlete, but I work bloody hard at my fitness. I sweat and work out at the gym and it's worth every minute of it. I might look knackered on the pitch and my body language might not be great, but you throw me the ball and I'll bowl for you all day.

Towards the end of 1997, there was talk that five members of the England party for the West Indies had failed a 'fatness' test and I thought, 'Christ, am I one of them?' Because I had put on a bit of weight at the end of the season. But I'll lose it before I go on tour. I know what I have to do. It's a fact that most players always end the summer heavier than when they started it – which might sound odd, but food and drink are put in front of you all summer wherever you go, whereas during the winter when you're at home, if you want something you have to get off your arse and do it yourself.

My brother Alastair, who played for Middlesex and Essex, is the opposite of me. He's built like an athlete and is naturally fit, but I put on weight easily and have to watch what I eat. Maybe I train more because I can lack discipline when I eat and drink, but I do take pride in my fitness. I always want to be among the fittest players at Middlesex and while that's the case, I'll know I can carry on playing. When the youngsters overtake me it will mean I've taken my foot off the pedal a bit, and that will be the time to worry.

I was aware of my hip during my 39 overs at Melbourne, but because things were going well, I just carried on. There wasn't a particular incident that made it go (although I do remember a match in Perth earlier in the tour when I fell on it and bruised it collecting a return near the wicket). Fact was, my problem was a cumulative thing.

Most of my six wickets that day came through frustration on the part of the batsmen. Certainly that was the case with Dean Jones, who played a dab shot at a ball he shouldn't have. Steve Waugh was bowled; Allan Border was strangled down the leg side; Ian Healy, who always likes to be positive, was out cutting; Greg Matthews was probably unlucky to be given out LBW, but so what; and then Alderman was also bowled. It was a flat surface and there wasn't a great deal of pace in it for the bowlers, but I bowled in the right areas and wore them down. They were trying to put the pressure back on me by taking the initiative away from me, but all they succeeded in doing was getting out.

Border's was my prize wicket that day and still is, probably more so than any other wicket I have taken in Test cricket. He is someone whom I admire greatly, a very hard man on the pitch who probably played the game a bit tougher than he should have done at times, but a great player who would never give you an inch. He was an absolute gentleman off the pitch, but he played the game to win and he and I had a couple of exchanges on the field over the years.

There was one time when he was playing for Essex in the Benson and Hedges Cup at Lord's and he was having a bit of a slog. He hit me for a couple of fours and then played and missed a couple of times, so I said something like, 'Why don't you hit it?' He replied that 'I've played against f****** better bowlers than you, mate,' and I was just about to say, 'Yes, and I've played against better batsmen than you', when I thought, 'Hold on a minute, I don't think I have.' So I just walked back to my mark and two balls later Border mowed me into the press box at Lord's in the Warner Stand, like a baseball hit. It went miles and I immediately thought that it served me right for taking the bloke on.

Then there was the time we played Australia, again at Lord's, in 1993, in what was a bad-tempered game. I'd had a run-in with Mike Gatting on the field, Gatt had had a further run-in with Micky Roseberry and then put his hand through a door, and I ended up being on the end of a real spanking. I bowled Border with a full toss near the end of their innings, which he had lost in the background – that often happens when you bowl from the Nursery End – and he just stood there as if to say the ball was over hip height and should have been a no-ball. When no call came from the umpire, I said, 'What are you hanging around for? You're out, f*** off.' Then Border started swearing back at me before turning around and wellying the other two stumps out of the ground. He got away with that, too.

Of course, Allan was great afterwards. I've met him often since then and we always get on well. I'd call him a great player. He was capable of destroying attacks even though he was not the most stylish of left-handers, like a Gower. He was a real fighter: the tougher it got, the more he rose to the challenge, and you had to battle to get his wicket. When Middlesex were talking about a coach to replace the retiring Don Bennett at the end of the 1997 season, Border's name was mentioned. I think he would be brilliant and there's no one I'd like to work with more. But I think he's not that keen to come over. Certainly, the way AB controlled and led the Australians was really impressive. We tend only to remember the glory years now, but he went through some tough times and there was a period in the mid 1980s when they were getting beaten regularly, yet he stuck to his guns and the way he thought was right to go about things. Border deserved everything that came his way and was the sort of cricketer Australians love. By the end of his tenure as captain, he had moulded the side exactly the way he wanted – and that legacy lives on today.

So we had bowled them out for 306, a lead of 46 for us, and again we'd played some good cricket but – as we often did on this tour – without cashing in. Denise always seems to be with me on tour when things have gone really well for me. Not that we could do much celebrating that evening – I was exhausted and had an early night.

Day four

Again we started our second innings well and, after losing Atherton early on, Gooch and Larkins took us to the stage where we were really fancying our chances. I wouldn't say the atmosphere in the dressing-room was relaxed, because it never really is, but we reached a point where we were almost saying, 'How much should we set them?' And that's fatal. The moment you start thinking like that is invariably the moment that it all goes bang, and the amount of times that's happened to me over the years is incredible. We were sitting there at lunch talking about what sort of target the Aussies could reach, then, all of a sudden after the interval, we were blown away. It was one of the most amazing collapses I've ever seen. Six wickets went for three runs as some really bad shots were played. Reid bowled well again, but not well enough to finish with seven for 51 and 13 wickets in the match. Just as at Brisbane, we blew it and left them with only 197 to get after slipping from 103 for one to 150 all out. All Reid had done was bowl a disciplined line and length and wait for the batsmen to make mistakes. It is a simple but effective way of picking up wickets.

I ended up walking back onto the field thinking that we should have been in a much stronger position. I'd bowled 39 overs in the first innings and needed more time off the field than four hours. I know you have to be fit enough to cope, but I'd thrown myself at it once and needed more time to recharge my batteries. I'd be lying if I said that sort of situation didn't affect you mentally. You don't go out with the same enthusiasm, because there's an air of inevitability about it all. You give it your best shot, of course you do, but you don't expect things to go as well again. It's rare for a bowler to produce the goods in both innings of a Test, like Reid did here. That's why there aren't many 'ten-fors' in Test cricket.

Having said that, even though we'd been skittled, we had a chance after having a good little session and reducing Australia to 28 for two at the close. We actually thought we could win the game at the end of a remarkable day.

Day five

It was not to be. We bowled well on the final day and had a couple of big decisions go against us, but could not take any more Australians down with us and lost by eight wickets. It was a hard day's cricket and Australia had the better of it, basically playing bloody well and outfighting us, Boon and Marsh being magnificent.

For me, though, another concern was that the hip was now very bad and making it intolerable for me to carry on. It had been an ache and pain that really hadn't affected my game, until now, when it became a biting pain in my right buttock which started during the morning session and got progressively worse as the day went on. I had to go off the field midway through the afternoon session because it had got so bad, but went back out later in case we took a few wickets, to make sure I was available to bowl. But it didn't happen for us.

When I walked off, the Aussie supporters had realised that I'd bowled myself into the ground for the cause and now couldn't bowl any more, so they gave me a standing ovation. It was something I didn't notice at the time because I was thinking about my hip and the fact that we were about to lose, but I was reminded of it by a book about the tour subsequently brought out by the *Daily Telegraph*, and it struck me how nice it was to have won the crowd over.

The supporters over there can be hostile. At times I found myself fielding in front of the infamous Bay 13 at fine leg, and to begin with they were giving me loads of stick – but when you laugh back and have a joke with them, you can sense that you're winning them over. There are always going to be idiots shouting out, 'Fraser, you loser, you're f****** useless,' or, 'Who's shagging your wife while you're over here? I hear she cooks a good breakfast.' They generally abuse you, but it got less and less as the match went on and by the end of it they seemed to respect me. It's like in the West Indies when people walk by you in the street and just say, 'Respect'. It's nice to be highly considered by the people you play in front of, particularly opposition supporters. On this occasion we had made their team work bloody hard for their runs, but they had proved better than us and now led the series 2–0.

We had played some good cricket but when it came to the crucial passages of play, they would always win them. They know when the moment is and seize it. It still happens now. Look at Trent Bridge in the 1997 season. Steve Waugh was out in the Aussies' second innings to give England a glimmer of hope but Healy came in and took the game away from them. It takes guts, but they do it and in an hour and a half the game's gone from you and there's nothing you can do about it. Good players know when the time is right to take a calculated risk, and the Melbourne

Test was there to be won by us until the Aussies snatched it away. My only consolation was some personal satisfaction with my own performance.

This match was Phil Tufnell's Test debut and he got off to an inauspicious start. He was not out nought in both innings and didn't get a wicket. There was also a run-in with an umpire which was clearly a sign of things to come!

Tuffers is a complex character. I knew him pretty well even then, because we came through the ranks together, and I've got to know him even better in the years that have followed, when he's developed into a fine bowler with the capacity for getting himself into trouble. He is a very accurate, disciplined bowler who is more knowledgeable about his art than people give him credit for. He can give the impression that he's not the brightest bloke in the world, but when he's got a ball in his hand he knows what it's all about. He can feel what the batsman is thinking – it must be a slow bowler's instinct – and can stand at the end of his run-up in the nets and say, 'He's going to charge me,' and the batsman does.

Phil can come across as not putting too much thought into his game, but he does. His views on cricket are very good and worth listening to, when he can be bothered to sit down and think about it. He has a reputation of being trouble and, fair enough, he has his moments and can be hard work to be with, but most of the time he's bloody good fun and can have everybody in stitches with his stories.

When he relates the scrapes he's been in – and he's been in a few – he's an absolute scream and I find him entertaining and amusing. I'm sure Tuffers will admit now that when he first came into the England side, the stardom did come a bit big to him and he got a bit carried away by it all. That actually affected him for a few years, but he has grown up and his wife Lisa, whom he met in the West Indies, is a big steadying influence on him. She controls him. And for the last two or three years, his game has been good and his actions, in the main, have been good, too.

He got off on the wrong foot with Gooch, there's no doubt about that. Tuffers is not the best trainer and doesn't like doing nets and fielding practice for the sake of it, so he can come across as being not fully committed all the time. That wound Graham up in Australia and he struggled a bit with him. They get on fine now, but then, with Tufnell fresh on the scene, you would have thought he would be the bright-eyed new boy and do whatever he was told. But even then he was a bit 'What are we doing this for?' and that used to upset Gooch.

In the second innings at Melbourne, Tufnell clashed with umpire Peter McConnell. There was a bit of tension throughout the day as Phil searched in vain for his first Test wicket. His appealing had obviously got to the umpire and when Phil asked him how many balls were left in a particular over, the umpire said, 'Count them your f****** self.' Tuffers didn't take that too well and reacted, so that eventually, Gooch got involved.

Then there was that business in the next Test at Sydney when Phil bowled really well and would have bowled England to victory if he had got the rub of the green with umpiring decisions. He had finally got his first Test wicket when Greg Matthews hit him to long-on and Tuffers turned to the umpire and appealed sarcastically, so frustrated had he become. Then he appeared to turn his back on Gooch and refused to shake hands with him as the captain tried to congratulate him. Tufnell's story was that he was so relieved to get the wicket, he just wanted to go to the fielder and shake his hand and hadn't realised who was around him, but it didn't look good at the time.

His fielding, too, became an issue on that trip. It's never actually been as bad as people thought after seeing him on that first tour, and he's always been an athletic character. When he tries hard he can be a bloody good fielder, but on this tour the crowds got to him over it and put him under pressure. He had no trouble settling in to bowling at Test level, but because he's not so confident about his fielding, the whole thing escalated until he was a bag of nerves every time the ball came to him.

It's not as if anyone who has captained Phil has had an incident-free reign. Mike Atherton has had some hard times with him and even Mike Gatting, who is acknowledged as having brought the best out of him, has had his shouting matches with Tufnell. Where Gatting did well was in realising early on that the bloke had a lot of talent and perhaps giving him more leeway than most. Under other captains, Tuffers might have been thrown out of cricket, because his job has been on the line a few times and even now, there's rarely a summer when there's not a couple of Tufnell incidents. But Gatting and Middlesex have been forgiving.

Personally, I don't like double standards. I don't like it when some players can get away with things and others can't, but I think with Tuffers over the years I've just accepted it. He's always been fit enough to do his job and get through his overs, even if he doesn't score too highly on the bleep tests. I've changed in the same corner of the dressing-room as him for 10 years, so we must get on pretty well and as long as Phil has a nice settled home life, a crucial factor for him, he's great company. There's certainly never a dull moment when Philip Clive Roderick Tufnell's about!

The interim

After Melbourne, it seemed to the outside world that I was prioritising one-day cricket ahead of Tests, but that wasn't true. Basically, I knew I could get through 10 overs with my hip problem but I also knew I couldn't get through 25 overs in a day or 40 overs in an innings, so I played in most of the one-dayers but didn't play in the Sydney Test. I wasn't put under extra pressure to play in limited-overs cricket. I wanted to do it because I wanted us to get something out of the tour. We were 2–0 down after two matches and I wanted to at least salvage something if the Ashes were to be lost.

In Sydney we were staying at a place called the Bondi Apartments, just up the road from Bondi Beach. They were pretty plush places but had one problem: cock-roaches. Every time you turned the lights on to go into a room, you would see them scurry for cover. I must say, you don't sleep too well when you know they are about. This made the kitchen a no-go area for the girls, Denise and Suzie (Mike Atherton's girlfriend at the time). I don't know whether their fear was genuine or just an excuse to get out of cooking, but it worked. New Year's Eve was spent at Doyles, a superb fish restaurant at Watson Bay. We saw the New Year in and left at 12.15, but stayed up until 2am at the apartment – Atherton, Tufnell and me talking cricket, much to the annoyance of our girlfriends, who had retired to bed. Fortunately, we could have a lie-in as the one-day game was a day-nighter that started at 2.30pm.

So I managed to play in the Sydney one-dayer on New Year's Day, which lived up to expectations, and had been regularly seeing the physio in an attempt to cure my injury. At that stage, I still didn't think it was that serious. You never tend to think the worst unless it's something you can see on X-rays and scans. You just hope it's a niggle that will go away. But I was certainly feeling down about everything.

Looking back in my diary now, I wrote that the team seemed lacklustre, just rolling along from one game to the next. I felt at the time that losing wasn't hurting some of my team-mates as much as it was others. I also wrote that we needed to sit down as a team to sort out some real problems with attitude. We did have a meeting and touched on our problems, but I felt some people were getting away with more than they should. There was a lot of soul-searching and we were asking ourselves why we weren't clicking and why we weren't playing well. The frustrations were coming out. We were under pressure. Losing isn't fun, and every game to us was getting bigger and bigger as criticism from the media began to grow. Some of the players didn't want extra practice sessions, but I could see why we had to do them. If you're not playing well, what else can you do except work hard to put it right? But there wasn't much time to do that. The Sydney Test was upon us.

I had a work-out before Sydney but the hip didn't feel right. I told Laurie Brown I didn't think I could get through a Test, and I knew it was the right decision. It was frustrating, because I was doing well when I was playing, but I wasn't up to it. It was like I'd pulled a big muscle in my backside. I knew, though, that the problem was in my hip joint because every time I turned over in the night, I'd wake up with a sharp pain in my right hip. And even though you know you shouldn't, you can't leave an injury alone when you've got one. It's a psychological thing. I used to feel it to see if it was still there and, of course, it was.

The team played well at Sydney. Gower got a superb hundred, much more like the real him, and Tufnell his first five-wicket haul in Test cricket. If a couple of decisions had gone our way, we could easily have won – it was a tense last day but at the end of it we had lost the Ashes, so that was that.

After a fairly commendable show at Sydney, however, there followed an awful performance in a match most of the players didn't want to play in. Because we hadn't qualified for the one-day finals, the management organised an extra game against New South Wales at Albury and we got stuffed by six wickets. A lot of the players felt that rest would have been more beneficial, and the mood of those who were there was made worse by the fact that some players had been given the match off. So the Test players were playing under duress and the others felt they were only playing because nobody else would. The end result was a game in which most people went through the motions.

Even that, though, caused us nowhere near as much grief as our next match. The game against Queensland was, actually, our only first-class win of the tour. But no one remembers that. What they remember was an incident that could easily have ended with two of our players being sent home for a practical joke that went badly wrong.

At a quiet moment of the game, with Lamb and Smith batting in our first innings, the peace was disturbed by the sound of two old aeroplanes flying low through the centre of the ground. On board were David Gower and John Morris, who had both seen their innings ended earlier. I can only think David must have been bored. He had scored hundreds in the last two Tests, had been excused duty at Albury and had got out cheaply here. We had seen these Tiger Moths flying around the area earlier in the day as part of an air display nearby, and then, all of a sudden, I was sitting there watching the game as twelfth man and this plane came down really low across the ground to salute Robin's century.

I said, 'That's a bit dangerous. Who's in there?' Peter Lush, the tour manager, was next to me and looked equally baffled – until we discovered later that two of our number were involved. I thought, 'God, what have they done? That can't have been them in there.' Especially with the way things were going for us. All right, it was a bit of fun, the guys in the middle loved it and those of us watching found it amusing, but there was no way it was going to be well-received, particularly as we had just lost the Ashes. Normally you have to ask permission from the captain to leave the ground during a match, but these guys had not only done that but had gone on a plane ride! God knows what would have happened if they had carried on with their plan to flour and water-bomb the players in the middle!

The enormity of it couldn't have hit them until later,

because they even posed for pictures with the planes before returning to the ground. It must have seemed like a good joke when they planned it and a few of the lads were in on it but had been sworn to secrecy. You could only imagine what sort of impression this gave out: that England didn't care about their predicament and just wanted to have a laugh. It certainly backfired on them, particularly John Morris, who never played for England again. His last innings for his country was 132 against Queensland. He hadn't had the best of tours up to then, but this business finished him off.

John knew he was in trouble, because he was threatening to deck anyone who was taking the mickey out of him about it. He had been summoned to a big meeting, but the lads, showing enormous 'sympathy', just shouted 'Bandits at six o'clock' whenever they saw him. David, meanwhile, was David and didn't appear to give a damn. When they were hauled in front of the management and fined £1,000 each, David even paid in cash straight away, in Australian dollars, so it wasn't taken out of his wages after they'd been taxed.

I couldn't believe they'd done it. I look back now and laugh, but at the time, we were playing awful cricket and were getting our arses kicked from pillar to post. It just looked so bad. I don't know whether the punishments fitted the crime, but I knew they'd get something. Gower was a former England captain who was supposed to be helping Gooch with the younger players, but in doing this he was trivialising our situation. Obviously the Gower lovers, who are in their millions, and the cavaliers loved it, but I don't think it set the right example. It also strained David's relationship with Gooch further – and that was before his infamous shot in Adelaide. More of which later.

So off we went to Adelaide for the fourth Test. The Ashes had gone and the atmosphere wasn't quite as intense as before. We hadn't achieved what we wanted to but we had to try to get something from the tour. And I had to decide if I was fit enough to play.

Fourth Test, Adelaide Oval; 25–29 January 1991

Day one

Our first morning warm-up at the Adelaide Oval had been accompanied by the theme from the Dambusters being played over the Tannoy – someone clearly had a sense of humour – but my mind was on my hip. I'd got through the one-day games and didn't know what to do. The hip didn't feel very good and I wrote in my diary that I didn't think I should play, but it was just about passable at the start of the day.

I wasn't going to go for it until I spoke with Micky, who really wanted me to play; so for the first time in a Test, we left Jack out of the side and asked Alec Stewart to keep wicket so that an extra bowler could play as cover for me. This, of course, has been a policy followed often since, as England's selectors have desperately searched for an all-rounder to give our side the balance it requires. It has always been a great shame for Jack, who was one of the last people who deserved to be dropped then and, more often than not, since then, too. He has been a victim of other people's poor form.

Australia won the toss and batted and my hip soon felt bad in the field, particularly after tea. I wondered even then if I was buggering my body up because it felt so sore, but at least we were doing quite well – until Mark Waugh got going. After tea, Waugh, on his debut, really took it away from us with a brilliant innings. Adelaide has a reputation for being flat, but there is usually something in it early on and so it proved on this occasion – until after tea. Mark Waugh was so composed it looked as though he had been in Test cricket for years. He didn't look nervous at all, just went out and did the business and looked bloody good, scoring 100 off just 124 balls. Australia, after being in a bit of trouble, were 269 for five at the close.

Since my injury, I have always thrown myself at my cricket with the attitude that I would see how my body shapes up at the end of it. If I have to have a hip replacement when I'm older, then so be it. I just hope the process is so far advanced that it will be, by then, a relatively easy operation. But I didn't feel that way in Adelaide in early 1991. Then, I was worried that it might be something serious and was concerned that it wasn't going to go away.

That didn't stop me giving my all in the fourth Test and I bowled quite well, beating the bat quite a bit, but I failed to take a wicket in 23 overs in Australia's first innings. I also went over on my ankle, coming round the wicket to a left-hander for the second time that winter, and twisted it so badly that I couldn't bowl on the second day. I was desperate to be fit because I thought it was my kind of wicket, one that if you put something in you'd get something out of it – but I wasn't getting as much out of it as the others.

Day two

Phil DeFreitas bowled well to get four wickets but the Aussies progressed to 386 before we dismissed them. Mark Waugh went for 138 in the end, one of the great debut innings; Devon bowled him. We then made reasonable progress to 95 for two by the close, with Gooch reaching his half century. You always felt more secure with him at the crease, but, as so often, the wheels were about to come off.

Day three

It was so obvious what the Aussies were trying to do to get David's wicket. Earlier during his innings, a few of their bowlers, particularly Merv Hughes, were bowling two or three feet down the leg side to him and he just kept on having one-handed flicks at the ball. He could so easily have made contact with them. Meanwhile, a couple of fielders were positioned on the leg side in case he should make contact, but we had only lost one wicket, that of Robin Smith, as we approached lunch, and a few of us started to make our way from the dressing-room to a spiral staircase which led down to where lunch was being served.

We stopped at the top of the staircase expecting to watch David play out the last over before the break, and were astonished when he hit Craig McDermott straight down Hughes's throat at deep square-leg. We just looked at each other and said, 'I don't believe it.' I don't know how well Gower and Gooch got on before the tour, but clearly their relationship was at a low ebb now. Graham walked off very quietly, as the not out batsman, while the Aussies couldn't believe their luck in trapping one of England's best players in this manner just before an interval. It wasn't exactly playing for lunch.

I don't think Graham said anything in the dressing-room to David when they came off. With Gower, there was no real point, because he was the way he was. But I'm pretty sure it was the last straw as far as Graham was concerned. Their relationship was tense throughout the tour because they are at such opposite ends of the scale in attitude. The Tiger Moth affair had put it under a lot of pressure – and now this. Graham was looking for David to play a responsible role on this tour, and then he plays a shot like that.

Now David Gower has achieved more in the game than I ever will, and you have to remember that he had scored two hundreds in our previous two Tests. You have to take him how he is. But on this occasion, nobody could believe the shot he had played. Gooch and Micky Stewart were adamant that the way forward for English cricket was based on hard work and discipline, and then such an influential figure has dropped it down deep square-leg's throat two minutes before lunch. It went against everything they were trying to achieve, which is why it was such a major thing.

David is a magnificent player and I get on well with him, but my approach to the game is different to his. I'm more in the Gooch mould. It's lovely to watch someone like David take the bowling apart but it's so frustrating when he gets out in a soft manner. He has always actually been a lot more serious about his cricket than a lot of people give him credit for, but he always makes it clear, also, that there is a lot more to his life than cricket. He was always going to enjoy himself on this tour. He's a legend in Australia and you didn't see as much of him as other players because he was often out with friends and was never short of things to do. He had a lifestyle that all of us envied, always being invited to go on a yacht round Sydney harbour or up the Swan river.

He has got a temper on him that can blow, but most of the time he's easy going, never throwing his bat around when he's out. He just used to sit in a corner of the dressing-room for a while, thinking about things and reflecting on what had happened. I found him a difficult man to get to know. He was different to most cricketers. It was hard to discover what really made David Gower tick, what his motivations were and what he was trying to achieve. I remember having a go at him in the field during this tour. He had dropped a straightforward catch soon after taking an amazing one, then he misfielded off me and I shouted at him. He looked at me as if to say: 'How can you bollock me?' A couple of overs later he made a brilliant stop off my bowling and I clapped him and said, 'Great fielding, David.' He said: 'I'm glad you said that, because I wasn't ready for the way you had a go at me earlier. I was going to have a word with you about what you said, but I'll let you off now.'

My attitude was that I couldn't treat him any differently just because he was David Gower. I've always had a go at fielders who misfield. It's frustration on my behalf as well as a bit of annoyance, but I'm on thin ice because I'm not exactly Jonty Rhodes in the field. It's all right for batsmen, they have control of their own destiny. But bowlers have to rely so much on fielders to help them get their wickets.

Obviously, David's methods worked for him because he had such a fine record, but Gooch had seen how a work ethic had worked for Allan Border and the Australians and he was trying to get England to do the same. I sympathised with him. The only time I saw David really upset at getting out was in the last Test at Perth when he fell 30-odd runs short of Geoff Boycott's record as leading English run-scorer in Test cricket. I actually think David would have retired after that match if he had broken the record, but as it was he hung around for another couple of years, which actually said a lot for him as he fought to get back into the side and deservedly reached the landmark against Pakistan. You always want to do well as a team, but you have personal goals, too. That record would have meant a lot to David and I'm sure he was determined to keep on going until he achieved it, even if it meant going back to Hampshire to play what, for him, was mediocre cricket.

So, David's wicket was the start of yet another collapse and we were all out for 229, a deficit of 157 runs. But by the close we had them 68 for four in their second innings and were competing again, after doing well in Sydney.

Day four

They didn't have any reason to give us a chance in this match – you don't risk defeat with a declaration in Test cricket – and batted us out of it on the fourth day. David Boon got a hundred and Border was not out 83 when the declaration came towards the end of play. We had been left the small matter of 471 to win and I had bowled another 26 overs while in discomfort. At least this time I'd got a wicket, but it was only that of nightwatchman Merv Hughes. So I ended the match with a solitary wicket, making me wonder whether I had made the right decision to play.

Day five

Gooch and Atherton went off like a train with the attitude that if we had a go, we might get somewhere close to our target. But it was far too high a mountain to climb. We could be pleased with a respectable 335 for five at the close, with Gooch scoring 117 to follow his first innings 87 and Atherton weighing in with 87. It wasn't a great Test performance, but not too bad.

Gooch's innings was another example of what a colossus he had become since being made captain. He was a tremendous batsman. I got on very well with him and still do. I feel I owe him a great deal – just watching him prepare for a game was educational. Blokes don't become that good through luck, they become that good by putting the effort in and Gooch was the perfect example of that. He was always a quiet, shy, undemonstrative man who just got on with his game. The opposition always wanted his wicket most, and he must have found it frustrating captaining our side and being as good as he was while we weren't doing as well as we should.

We weren't exactly letting him down, but I sensed he wanted to get away from us at times because we were frustrating him. I think he felt some players were not as motivated as he was and he struggled at times to find out what made certain individuals tick, and how to get the best out of them. But that has been a recurring problem in English cricket and I remember speaking to Graham about it several times. He wanted to get the best out of people and asked me what more he could do. I don't think I was much help.

As a player and captain he was quite like Mike Gatting in that because he was such a good player of spin himself, he tended not to rate spinners that highly and preferred seam-oriented attacks. A lot of good players are like that – I remember Desmond Haynes saying to me: 'Why should I lose any sleep about facing someone who's bowling at 20 mph? He can't hurt me.'

Gooch believed in me and I earned his respect. As far as I'm concerned, there's no blame attached to him for my injury problems. As I've said, I wanted to bowl.

For me, Graham was in better form in this match than when he scored 333 at Lord's the previous summer. He got us to the point where we needed seven an over after tea, but we lost a few wickets and had to shut up shop. I had a cortisone injection on my hip after play and had X-rays which showed there was nothing structurally wrong. But after coming through this match, I didn't know whether to carry on and play in Perth.

The aftermath

In the end, there was just no point. Phil Newport flew in to replace me because the cortisone hadn't worked and my hip was still sore to the touch. We were hammered in the last Test by nine wickets to lose the series 3–0. It was a sad end to such a disappointing trip. We had continually got our-selves into good positions, only to blow it. I headed back to England thinking that I had two and a half months to get my body right and I was sure that would be enough. How wrong I was.

My biggest problem was finding out what was actually wrong with me. I effectively spent two years getting to the root of the trouble and getting the right diagnosis. Once I actually found out what was wrong, it wasn't that major a thing to cure. It was just some wear and tear in the hip joint and I eventually saw a specialist in Cambridge who cleared out the junk and debris and that was that. It was as simple as that in the end and immediately I had the operation, in 1993, I could feel the difference.

If only I had come back from Australia and seen that surgeon and had the advice he gave me, I'm sure I would have only missed half a season at most. It's frustrating, but

I can't be annoyed with the people I saw before him, because they were all trying their best on my behalf. I'm not going to blame anyone; they were trying to get me right and it wasn't through lack of effort that they failed. It was just that the condition I had was very rare for a bowler and it wasn't something that jumped out and presented itself to the specialists. It was only a period of trial and error that pinpointed it.

There were various stages when I thought my career was over. I had one big op at an early stage, open hip surgery, but that didn't cure it. I played in a couple of games early in the 1991 home season and then another surgeon came up with a wrong diagnosis, so I ended up missing most of that season. That didn't stop the selectors picking me for that winter's tour of New Zealand and the World Cup, mainly because I was one of their contracted players and they wanted to give me every chance of making it, but I, along with Mike Atherton, had to drop out when it was clear we couldn't make it.

At one point, I was wearing electric underpants because they said there was a dead area at the end of my femur (a vascular necrosis) and they thought that wearing those things would stimulate the blood flow. It didn't work. I was just going round on a tour of surgeons, which included the hip surgery in Nottingham and another disappointment. At the start of 1992, I decided to play through the pain, doing myself no justice at all, because I feared it was as good as it was ever going to be. It was a terrible year and I was at my lowest ebb.

Then I saw Mr R Villar, who performed an arthroscopy on my hip in Cambridge, and turned up for the 1993 season feeling good and my career took off again. That was not before a frustrating first half of the season when the initial novelty of being back as a force in first-class cricket soon began to wear off. You get to the point where you want to get back in contention for England again because county cricket is not enough, and that's exactly what I did do after a purple patch which saw me take 32 wickets towards the end of that campaign. I was back. I was selected for the final Test of the summer against the Australians at The Oval, when I took eight wickets and gained my first Test Man of the Match award. I had to wait until the third Test in Trinidad in 1998 for my second.

It was a magnificent match for me. It was so satisfying, after all I'd been through, to be back up there again. I got Mark Waugh out with a good ball and it was as happy a moment as my first Test wicket. When I made my debut, my career had been progressing well and it was as if Test cricket was meant to happen, but having got back to the top after being on the verge of quitting, the game was extra-special.

I do have one criticism of the surgeons who treated me. There seemed to be a lot of jealousy around the medical profession and it sometimes seemed almost a case of 'If I can't get you right, I don't want anyone else to, because it would reflect badly on me.' Sometimes my X-rays weren't released, stuff like that. But I refused to accept opinions that my outlook was poor and I wouldn't play professional cricket again. I wanted to see someone with a more optimistic view. I wouldn't say that seeing the man in Cambridge was the last throw of the dice, but it was pretty close to it. There are only so many instances of bad news that you can take.

So many people helped me through the bad times;

people like Patrick Whittingdale, who first offered to fly me to America for treatment and then gave me a job while I was trying to get back. But I went through some really low times. I am only trained to be a cricketer. It's what I always wanted to do and it's what I enjoy doing. What else could I do? It was in danger of being taken away from me.

Ricky Ellcock had finally retired after battling with his back problems and we had become very close. We'd talk about buying a plot of land in Barbados with our insurance money and putting houses on it. Anything, at the time, to give me hope for the future. I think I was pretty difficult for Denise to live with, too. I felt sorry for myself. But it all came right in 1993. My son Alex was born, I got back in the England side, initially as stand-by for Martin Bicknell but then in my own right, and then, on the last day of the Oval Test, I proposed to Denise after getting my Man of the Match award. So I must have been happy, to do that!

And then I earned myself a place on that winter's tour of the West Indies, against all pessimistic predictions. A tour place can mean so much to a cricketer. Just before I was picked, Denise was preparing to return to work after having Alex, because we couldn't survive on my Middlesex salary. But with a tour place, my winter financial expectations went up from the potential of earning £5,000 to £40,000. It's an insecure life, but very satisfying when it all comes together.

England to Australia 1990–91

First Test
Woolloongabba, Brisbane, 23, 24, 25 November
England 194 (D.I.Gower 61) and 114 (T.M.Alderman 6 for 41)
Australia 152 and 157 for 0 (G.R.Marsh 72 not out, M.A.Taylor 67 not out)
Result: Australia won by 10 wickets.

Second Test
Melbourne Cricket Ground, 26, 27, 28, 29, 30 December
England 352 (D.I.Gower 100, A.J.Stewart 79, W.Larkins 64, B.A.Reid 6 for 97) and 150 (G.A.Gooch 58, W.Larkins 54, B.A.Reid 7 for 51)
Australia 306 (A.R.Border 62, M.A.Taylor 61, A.R.C.Fraser 6 for 82) and 197 for 2 (D.C.Boon 94 not out, G.R.Marsh 79 not out)
Result: Australia won by 8 wickets.

Third Test
Sydney Cricket Ground, 4, 5, 6, 7, 8 January
Australia 518 (G.R.J.Matthews 128, D.C.Boon 97, A.R.Border 78, D.M.Jones 60) and 205 (I.A.Healy 69, P.C.R.Tufnell 5 for 61)
England 469 for 8 dec (D.I.Gower 123, M.A.Atherton 105, A.J.Stewart 91, G.A.Gooch 59) and 113 for 4 (G.A.Gooch 54)
Result: Match drawn.

Fourth Test
Adelaide Oval, 25, 26, 27, 28, 29 January
Australia 386 (M.E.Waugh 138, G.R.J.Matthews 65) and 314 for 6 dec (D.C.Boon 121, A.R.Border 83 not out)
England 229 (G.A.Gooch 87, R.A.Smith 53, C.J.McDermott 5 for 97) and 335 for 5 (G.A.Gooch 117, M.A.Atherton 87, A.J.Lamb 53)
Result: Match drawn.

Fifth Test
W.A.C.A.Ground, Perth, 1, 2, 3, 5 February
England 244 (A.J.Lamb 91, R.A.Smith 58, C.J.McDermott 8 for 97) and 182
Australia 307 (D.C.Boon 64, G.R.J.Matthews 60 not out) and 120 for 1 (G.R.Marsh 63 not out)
Result: Australia won by 9 wickets.

Angus Fraser's tour (1st, 2nd and 4th Tests):
Batting: 5 innings, 0 not out, high score 24, runs 27, average 5.40.
Bowling: 143 overs, 31 maidens, 311 runs, 11 wickets, average 28.27, best 6–82.

england in west indies 1993-94

The background

One of the most common things that has been written about me since I returned after injury is that I've never quite been the same bowler since, that I haven't got my old nip. To me, this is absolutely wrong.

I've twice improved my career best since returning to the big time at the end of 1993, and that has been in a period when the game has been more loaded in favour of the batsman, with flatter wickets and a smaller seam on the ball, than it was when I was at my 'peak'. When I retire and sit down to look back at what I have achieved, I might be able to accept that I wasn't quite the same after my hip problem, but now, I think I'm being honest in saying that I'm still the force I was.

You'd think I never did anything wrong before the injury, but if you look at my figures, I think you will see that there were times when I was pretty innocuous. I go into every Test match believing I can succeed and to do that I've got to believe I'm still as strong as ever. If I'm not as good now as I was before 1991, then I can't see it and I can't feel it.

Things were pretty good at the end of 1993. I was suddenly about to earn reasonable money again – money is not the be-all and end-all but it can change your life dramatically – and I was off to the West Indies for a second time. It was like a fresh start and I was determined to enjoy it, because it was such a bonus. This time, of course, I was to be touring for the first time under the captaincy of Mike Atherton, a player I'd struck up a friendship and a rapport with, mainly when we were both recovering from serious injury in 1992. I was only playing my third Test when, in 1989, he made his debut, so we were in the same boat then and I enjoyed his company. At that time, Alastair, my brother, knew Mike better than I did because he'd played youth cricket with him; but once I had got to know Athers we got on very well, and even though his decisions have at times tested our friendship, it has survived.

The prospect of having a younger man in charge created a different feeling. It was almost like the start of a new era again. Just as in 1990, we were putting faith in young players and telling them they had time to prove their worth, basically copying the Australian way. It was music to a lot of ears. Our trip became the most enjoyable I've ever been on, partly because I did well but also because the tour party was the nicest group of cricketers I've been away with. Everyone got on well and there were good lads like Steve Watkin and Alan Igglesden included, who fitted in really well.

We went to Lilleshall again and also had a week at the Barrington's resort in Portugal – once again the three-month break between the end of the season and the start of the tour was hugely beneficial – and we went to the West Indies having done the hard work in terms of preparation. We knew we were in for a tough series, but even before we left you could sense the feeling of 'Hang on, we could do well here.'

The build-up

We left home on 15 January, this time starting off in Antigua, and I went up into the cockpit for the take-off of our British Airways flight, which was an enjoyable experience. We stayed at the Halcyon Cove hotel, which is right on the beach and a fabulous place to be based. We worked hard in practice and the only minor hiccup came when Chris Lewis shaved his head as part of his deal to model Oakley sunglasses and promptly got sunstroke. I actually like Chris, but on this occasion I thought, 'You soppy sod. We're here to play cricket, not get involved in PR.'

The warm-up games went OK and we played pretty well, but I broke my finger in Barbados when Vasbert Drakes hit me while I was batting as a nightwatchman. I finally got out to Dale Maynard, a fast bowler whose trademark was always bowling with a toothpick in his mouth, and as I was sitting around the dressing-room area nursing my knuckle, both he and Drakes had an argument as to who had injured me. It was like another chalkmark on the wall for them. I said, 'Don't worry about me, will you!' Our injury problems were heightened the day before the first one-day international when Igglesden got pinned on the forearm by a local net bowler, and at one stage England were wondering who was going to bowl for them!

We won that one-dayer, Atherton batting well, and celebrated by staying up all night. Our flight left early, so we had to be up by 6.30am. By 2.30, a few of us thought, 'What's the point of going to bed?' So we stayed up chatting. The first Test in Jamaica, however, proved to be different and was a very hard match. I was still missing through injury and could only watch some very intense and intimidating cricket. Indeed, one of the best and most enthralling spells of cricket I have ever seen occurred when Courtney Walsh was bowling to Atherton in our second innings. Mike only got 28 but I can't believe he has ever had to be as strong on the field of play as he was that day.

Walsh really threw everything at him and Mike showed enormous pluck and fight. The captain, who hadn't been in the job long at that stage, really went up in the players' estimation for the way he withstood that onslaught. He couldn't have done any more to repel Walsh than he did, and we thought, 'If this bloke is prepared to go through all that, then he's the right man to lead us.' It was frightening, really, and almost moving, too. I don't know what the traditionalists would have thought about such raw, aggressive cricket, but for those of us watching that day it was heroic, compelling stuff.

Which was why Walsh's subsequent spell to Devon Malcolm later in that innings was so disappointing. Courtney seemed to be aiming straight at one of the worst batsmen in world cricket, going round the wicket to Devon at one stage and risking injuring him. I wrote in my diary at the time: 'Having bowled so well at Athers, what Walsh did to Devon was totally out of order. It just took away all the good that he did. His bowling to Athers was perfectly legitimate intimidation and what he did to Devon was ridiculous. The umpires were a waste of time.'

If I'd been Devon, I would have been gunning for Courtney when he had a bat in his hand for the rest of the series, but Devon's such a gentleman that he didn't give any back, even though he was visibly shaken by it all. Their intent was to knock him out of the way and it was disappointing and unnecessary.

The other significant aspect of that match, which we ended up losing by eight wickets, was Graeme Hick's knock of 96 in our second innings. I remember going out, as twelfth man, to take something to him when he was on 94, and he told me he would pay a million pounds for the extra six runs. He meant it, too. It was such a shame, then, when he fell to a great catch from Roger Harper, the substitute fielder. A lot of other fielders would have struggled even to get a hand to it, but Harper is one of the best around.

We then lost a one-dayer in Jamaica which was notable, as far as I was concerned, for me being sent off the field by my captain! I'd bowled my allocation of overs, not particularly well, in a rain-affected game in sweltering heat after returning from my hand injury, and Atherton said: 'You've bowled your overs, what are you doing out here?' I replied, 'I'm playing, that's what.' I'd just taken a good catch, too, but he said, 'We'll get you off and get a good fielder in your place. You pretend you've got hamstring trouble.' So out came the physio and I had to lie on my back having my hamstring stretched, pretending I was injured. Then, when I went off, I sat in the dressing-room on a towel of ice in case any West Indians stuck their heads around the door. The irony was that after I went off, the wheels came off and we lost! My alleged lack of mobility in the field has led to other captains suggesting this course of action, but apart from on that occasion, I've always told them to p*** off.

The rest of the one-day series went badly for us and we lost it 3–2. During this time, I'd been negotiating on a bat deal with Slazenger and Denise was trying to sort out the details from home. But they weren't being very co-operative and in the end she said, 'I'm not dealing with them any more.' So I ripped the Slazenger stickers off my bat and put 'Hi, Mum' in their place instead, for the benefit of the stump camera. I asked the match referee Sunil Gavaskar if it was OK and he said yes, as long as you're sure there's no company in the world called Hi Mum. I was sat there with us being thrashed at St Vincent waiting to go in to bat when Keith Fletcher, who was now the England manager, said, 'What's that on your bat?' He went mad, saying, 'Get that off your bat straight away, we're in enough shit without you bringing more attention to us.' I got stumped off Lara for one, so I probably wasn't in for long enough for my mum to have got the message anyway. This was also the match in which Phil Tufnell literally got slogged onto the runway alongside the cricket ground, so St Vincent wasn't a very happy trip for us.

But at least we won the last one-dayer and moved on to Guyana to play a West Indies Board President's XI, where we batted very well on a flat pitch. It was a good practice game. The batsmen got runs and the bowlers got a good bowl, but it didn't seem to do us much good in the Guyana Test because we were stuffed again. Our first-innings effort of 322 wasn't a bad score but it should have been more, because the pitch was an absolute belter. Curtly Ambrose bowled magnificently to take four wickets in each innings and was the only bowler to get something out of the pitch, showing again why he's the bowler he is.

Atherton batted very well for 144 and Robin Smith got 84, but then it all went downhill for us. Brian Lara by this time had earned himself a big reputation and he lived up to it by scoring a big hundred in this game. Jimmy Adams lent good support and the West Indies won by an innings. In 1990, of course, we hadn't bowled a ball in Guyana because of the weather and this time, when it was all going horribly wrong, I made a little entry in my diary which simply said: 'No sign of the rain yet!' We had competed fairly well in Jamaica, but we had been outplayed here and the West Indies simply had too much power for us. It meant that we went to Trinidad for the third Test 2–0 down and facing a very different position to that which we had earned when I was here with England in 1990.

Third Test, Queen's Park Oval, Port-of-Spain, Trinidad; 25–30 March 1994

Day one

The Queen's Park Oval is the biggest ground in the West Indies. It's a very nice place to play because it's very noisy and, from a bowler's point of view, the pitch gets a bit uneven, which is a help. But it's also very tropical and humid and, as the humidity always gets to me, I find Trinidad can be very hard work.

If we were going to do anything in this series, we felt, we were going to have to do it now. We had picked a young side because we thought that was the best way to go, but we had to justify it by being more consistent. We had a clear strategy but that didn't mean we had an indefinite amount of time to produce the goods. The captain let it be known that he would not muck about. He would make the decision to drop people if he had to. He was frustrated that we were two down, but we deserved to be. Again, in patches, we had played really well, but we hadn't seemed to be able to do it often enough. We had to get it right.

By this time in the series, we were becoming very confused about the policies being adopted by Richie Richardson, the West Indies captain. He always seemed to do the opposite of what we expected when he won the toss. In Guyana they bowled when we were sure they would bat, and now they batted when, really, it seemed a clear case of putting the opposition in.

We felt Richardson was giving us the best of the conditions and we did pretty well on that first day. We reduced them to 227 for seven by the close and it could have been better if Athers, or the 'dopey captain' as I called him that night in my diary, had not dropped Desmond

Haynes off my bowling early on. We bowled well as a side, but nothing really went our way before tea. After the break it went a lot better and we picked up six wickets in the last session. I got some return for my efforts, bowling Shivnarine Chanderpaul and Winston Benjamin, and we had shown that if we kept the pressure on, as the 1990 team did, then wickets would come.

Day two
Our good work continued in the morning when we got rid of the remaining wickets quickly to bowl the West Indies out for 252. I dismissed Ambrose and Kenny Benjamin to end with four, as did Chris Lewis, but Atherton's dropping of Haynes not only denied me a 'five-for' but proved costly in another way, too. Ever since we first toured together, Mike and I have had this bowlers-versus-batsmen argument. I always tell him it's the batsmen who let England down, while he tells me that all our problems are down to the bowlers. So by this time, we had started having a side bet each time we toured, as to who, in his case, would score the most centuries or, in mine, take most 'five-fors' during the course of the series. On this occasion he won 2–1, but if he'd caught that absolute knob-ender to get rid of Haynes, it would have been 2–2. As it was, I had to buy him a meal at the end of the tour.

Our performance was also, as far as I was concerned, the perfect answer to some criticism we had been receiving in the local press. Colin Croft, that most fearsome of fast bowlers and now, among other things, a media pundit, had torn into us in print while we were in Guyana, questioning Hick's courage against fast bowling and saying that I reminded him of an old carthorse who should be put out to grass. Now we'd bowled them out for 252 – not bad for what Croft considered the worst bowling attack in Test cricket. We didn't, however, forget his words. Later on in the tour, when we were in Barbados, we returned to the dressing-room to find a bat to be autographed waiting for us. We asked who it belonged to and the attendant said it was Colin Croft's. That was the cue for Alan Igglesden, who had also received some stick from him, to pick it up, unsigned, and throw it out of the dressing-room window.

If there was an England batsman under threat after the first two Tests, it was Graham Thorpe. But the selectors showed faith in him and he repaid them with an excellent innings in our reply. He was unbeaten on 64 at the end of the second day and we were well pleased to reach 236 for five. Our progress was quite slow, with occupying the crease being the priority, but that was how we had done well in 1990 and now Graham and Jack Russell dug in for two hours to lift us close to the West Indies' score with five wickets remaining. We felt that by being defensively minded, we could knock the stuffing out of them.

Day three
We all did pretty well with the bat. Thorpe led the way with 86 but even one ARC Fraser chipped in with an unbeaten eight. It meant that we had got up to 328 all out, a lead of 76 and a springboard for a victory bid. But how often have we squandered chances like this? Everything seemed to be going our way when the West Indies batted again, even though, for some reason I can't put my finger on, I didn't bowl very well at all.

The last session was particularly good for us. Everything went our way, including what we thought at the time was the potentially crucial wicket of Jimmy Adams, in bizarre circumstances right at the end of the day. Ian Salisbury had bowled Adams a big full 'bunger' and he smashed it straight at short leg Robin Smith's arm and the rebound was snapped up by Jack. That incident really made us think that the gods were smiling on us and that the game was swinging our way. We had 'won' all three days of the match so far and the West Indies were 143 for five, 67 ahead with just five wickets to go. We were in a bloody good position and we went into the rest day well pleased with our efforts and looking to wrap the game up from here. Everybody was thinking positively.

Day four
Rarely can everything have gone so badly for a team who appeared to be in a match-winning position. For a start, Graeme Hick, such a reliable slip fielder, dropped Chanderpaul, the West Indies' last recognised batsman who had started the day unbeaten on one, twice; once very early on when he was on four. There was no real explanation for it. People started to think Hick wasn't as sharp at slip to the left-handers, but he had taken them there before and went on to do so again. Those two misses, however, were unquestionably vital ones. Chanderpaul went on to make 50 priceless runs and managed to guard the West Indies tail to productive effect.

It was such a frustrating morning trying to finish them off. At one point we had a break for rain and the dressing-room was quite tense, because we could see the game slipping out of our grasp. Then, I have to confess, I 'trollied', the cricketing term for losing your rag. I had told Mark Ramprakash that someone wanted to see him outside the dressing-room, so that I could nick his seat – a silly prank of the kind that you often do to pass the time away in these situations. When he came back, having found no one outside, he picked up my England cap and threw it into some water. With something as valuable as your cap you can get a bit protective and I booted a bin across the dressing-room and squared up to Ramps in the middle of the room. It was stupid, but it was me showing my irritation at not bowling well and letting the pressure of the situation get to me. I felt that it was drifting away from us after we had done so well.

But we started to pull it back when we went back out. I took two catches, one each off Andrew Caddick and Chris Lewis, and Andy finished up with six for 65 as we bowled them out for 269, leaving us 193 to win and a tricky little evening session to negotiate in far from ideal light. Nobody, however, could be prepared for what was about to follow.

We had 20 overs left of the day and the whole of the following day to score 193, so really our only priority was to get through to the close with as little damage done to us as possible. We knew it might be tough, though, because Ambrose and Walsh would be running in hard and 193 was never going to be easy to get. Consequently, we all felt very nervous as we prepared to watch our innings begin. I was just getting changed after finishing bowling when I looked up to watch the first ball on the dressing-room television. Things could not have started worse. The first ball from Ambrose thudded into Atherton's pads and he was palpably LBW. I just thought, 'Oh, no.' Mike came in, utterly dejected, but we were all still concentrating on the TV.

In the same over, Mark Ramprakash was run out after a horrible mix-up with Alec Stewart and the captain buried his head in a towel and screamed, 'No, no, no.' What followed was like nothing I had ever seen on a cricket field before (or since). It was a combination of pressure, panic and terrific bowling. The tenseness of the situation had got to people and it made for unbelievable viewing. Just being sat there looking at everybody was too much for me and I had to get out of the dressing-room. So I went with Chris Lewis for a walk round the ground to a roti stall to get something to eat. Only we never made it that far.

As we were about to leave, Robin Smith had his off stump knocked out of the ground and Hick went soon after. Just as we reached the Kentucky Fried Chicken stall, Stewart was out, our top scorer with 18, so Chris had to hurriedly return to the dressing-room to get padded up. I, meanwhile, abandoned the quest for a roti and settled for a KFC, bringing Chris something to eat in the dressing-room.

The Queen's Park Oval dressing-rooms provide a horrible little viewing area. Everybody is huddled up on a little balcony behind the bowler's arm and it's an intense spot. You can see all of what's going on and there's a passionate crowd on one side of you. It's very close to the action, but as a player, you prefer to be cut off from it all when you're not involved. There was all the excitement, the sea of faces and the noise. The banging as Ambrose ran up to bowl. The sound just got louder and louder as each of our wickets fell one by one, rapidly, after each other.

We just crumbled completely. Ambrose was sensational. At the close we were 40 for eight, and I couldn't get the image of Graham Thorpe's face, completely fazed with almost horror etched into it, which filled the TV screen in the dressing-room after he had been bowled by Ambrose just before the close, out of my head. We really were like rabbits caught up in headlights. The conditions were good for Ambrose but he just worked everything up into a fever pitch. We were trapped in a very intimidating environment with nowhere to go.

Ambrose got all six of his wickets that night in one of the most famous pieces of fast bowling in history, and was carried off the pitch by frenzied supporters. We had simply been blown away. Later on I watched the video of this tour which was compiled by Jonathan Agnew with Atherton for the BBC and it brought it all back. They showed us all getting on the team bus at the Trinidad Hilton, the upside down hotel, on that fourth morning, so buoyant and so up for the day ahead. We had all told the camera that we were going to do it – we had all been full of such hope. Then the video showed us all getting back on the bus after the evening's play, looking absolutely devastated. There were also pictures of us sitting in a row at the end of it all and I don't think I've ever seen such desolation. We had 'won' the first three days of the match but everything had gone wrong on the fourth, most particularly in that amazing final session, and we were looking at one of the lowest totals in Test cricket.

My brother Alastair was in Trinidad at that time with a group of friends, so I went to see him that night to get away from it all. There seemed little point in moping around. All that was left were the final rites the next morning.

Day five
Courtney Walsh took the last two wickets to fall, leaving us all out for 46 and me unbeaten without scoring – so they couldn't blame me for the debacle! The hero for the West Indies, however, was undoubtedly Ambrose. We had lost

the game in an hour and he is one of the few players capable of turning a whole match around like that. He will go down as one of the greats.

I don't know if the young Curtly Ambrose even wanted to play the game that much. He came onto the scene quite late and had spent much of his youth as a basketball player, which is still, I believe, his great sporting love. He just happened to have an enormous talent for cricket and eventually realised he would have to do something with it. He first came to England in 1988 and bowled quickly even then, immediately looking a class act. He has been one ever since.

As a bowler, Curtly is everything I would wish to be. He's consistent, accurate and hostile. For instance, he bowled a couple of balls at Jack Russell in our ill-fated second innings that were absolute lightning. The first one cleaned him up and the second left him so fazed that he was on his way soon afterwards. Ambrose has the ability to bowl genuinely quick balls, but most of the time, he bowls within himself – still at a good pace – and then steps it up and bowls an effort ball a yard quicker. He bowled a few effort balls that night in Trinidad, and they really shook us.

Curtly is a man with great pride. In the next match, in Barbados, he got smashed around a bit, which must have been a shock to his system, but he kept on running in and didn't ever give up on the game. He is one of the best there has been. His control is exceptional and he's mainly a seam bowler, getting very little swing. A few times during Tests, I will go out at lunchtime to look at the pitch and see what length the bowlers are hitting. On this tour, you could see Ambrose's length straight away. People go on about swing and pace, and yes, they're great to have, but you also have to pitch the ball in the right area and Curtly does it again and again. He just so rarely bowls bad balls, just keeps banging away wearing the bastards down. If there's a bit in the wicket he'll get it out, but if there's not he's still a handful because he automatically bowls in the right areas. Someone of 6ft 7in is always going to be the man to watch, to see what he does with the ball, where he pitches it and how he moves it. It's a simple process. Glenn McGrath's the same. The best bowlers are very uncomplicated in their methods. All right, Ambrose and McGrath are both tall men, but I try to bowl like them. They've both got a yard or two of pace on me which is why, unfortunately, they've been a bit more successful than me – but the method behind our bowling and what we are trying to achieve are the same.

Ambrose has been a figure of controversy in some ways and has supposedly caused a bit of trouble in the West Indies dressing-room from time to time. But to me, even though he is a formidable, intimidating figure with a cricket ball in his hand, he has been fine. Like all West Indians, he doesn't go in for sledging, preferring to just give you that famous, almost theatrical look of his if you upset him. He burst out laughing once when I tried to slog him and succeeded only in toe-ending the ball to gully, but I've always got on well with him. He was more than happy to do an article for my benefit brochure and the copy arrived promptly without me having to chase him up. John Emburey has told me that Curtly was very good in the Northants dressing-room when he was there. He wants to play, he works and trains hard, he's a fit man and he wants to take responsibility. At Middlesex, Emburey used to be called 'the King' because he caught everything that came his way on an England tour to Australia in 1986–87. Then, when John moved to Northants, he found their players used to call Ambrose the same. Whenever they called Curtly, John would turn around until, eventually, he had to accept that Curtly was 'the King', not him.

I know the press won't agree with me – he never talks to them – but Curtly seems good fun. Whenever I see him he always seems to be laughing and joking with his team-mates, and these rumours about him causing trouble among them might have been started because he is one of the few in their team who will stand up to Brian Lara. Curtly is amusing to talk to and has a typical bowler's attitude to the game. He thinks it's hard work and is always saying he's had enough and is going to retire, complaining that they're always changing the rules to make it easier for batsmen and harder for him to do his job. Then, just when you think you've seen the last of him, up he pops again; so deep down, he must care for the game really.

When he walked off at The Oval in the last Test of the 1995 season and turned and saluted the crowd, I really thought that was the last we'd see of him. I even talked to him about him packing it all in, but there he was again that winter and he's still going now. He must be like me – towards the end of a hard series, you think to yourself, 'There must be easier ways to earn a living than this,' but then you go away for a couple of months and come back wanting it even more. It's certainly very dangerous to write him off. People say he's not the bowler he once was and that could very well be true, but he's still a very fine one. He'll be very proud to have reached 300 Test wickets, I know that – and who's to say there won't be many more before he's finished?

The interim

Trinidad wasn't the end of our troubles, by any means. From there we went on to Grenada, where we experienced one of the worst tour games I have ever known. It was a horrible, end-of-tour thing. The blokes who had done well in the Tests didn't have to play, and those who came in felt they were only forced into it because no one else wanted to play. It's a common problem towards the end of a tour and one that I can't really think of an answer for.

We played a West Indies Board XI and were stuffed again. We played poor cricket, we lacked motivation and there was no real atmosphere about the game. We only had two days off after Trinidad, which wasn't good, and the whole thing was very depressing. Ramprakash got runs, which was something, as did Hick, but we deserved nothing better than our eight-wicket defeat. At this time, we were all very low, 3–0 down in the series and in danger of another 'blackwash'. I can't think of any one incident which lifted our spirits or changed things around for us, but we were about to undergo a complete transformation and pull off one of England's best wins in Test cricket. It was quite a turnaround.

Fourth Test, Kensington Oval, Bridgetown, Barbados; 8–13 April 1994

Day one

The wives and girlfriends had arrived on tour, which might have had something to do with cheering us up a bit – I think their presence took our minds off the 'horror' of Trinidad. You can get too wrapped up and intense about things at times, and I certainly didn't really think about the Test until it was virtually upon us.

On the night before the match, Alex, my little boy, had a bad night and woke up at 5am, so I had to sleep on the sofa for an hour and a half; not the most glamorous of preparations for such a big game. The wicket looked a bit damp at the start, but it only seamed for an hour or so at most. Even so, there was enough potentially in it for the West Indies to win the toss and stick us in to bat. Now, though, things went better for us. There were so many Englishmen in the ground that their mere presence picked us up immediately and it was almost like being at home. I say almost, because in England the supporters' behaviour is very sedate and people don't want them to get involved in the game. Abroad, though, it is totally different. The England supporters are very vocal and get carried along by the excitement generated by the locals. All players enjoy playing in this sort of atmosphere. They get you going, you feel they are behind you – and they certainly were here.

Away supporters really were in the majority, which was amazing, particularly as we were 3–0 down at the time. When you're in Guyana, you feel so far from home and in such a different culture that you know you're on tour, but not here. A lot of the poor Barbadians were struggling to get tickets for their own Test, such was the demand for them among British tour operators. Such familiar surroundings make it easier for you to lead a normal life and enjoy the luxuries of the Caribbean. It was just an environment I felt totally at home with.

We desperately didn't want another 5–0 series defeat – something we were looking down the barrel of – and we now faced a real test of our character. How were we going to react? Desmond Haynes was apparently very keen on the local groundsman producing a green, spiteful wicket for this one to try to shove it up us even more – the nasty sod! – but it actually turned out to be a good surface and we started well on it.

Mike Atherton was the first man to go, to a loose shot, but not before we had 171 on the board and the captain had contributed 85 of them. But then our near-perfect start to the day was partially spoiled when we lost four wickets in the last session. Ramprakash was caught behind, as was Robin Smith, who got a good ball from Winston Benjamin. Stewart, on his 31st birthday, scored a hundred before being caught by Brian Lara off Kenny Benjamin, and Thorpe went cheaply before the close. Even so, we were 299 for five, having fought well and had a pretty good first day.

Day two

We didn't get the start we were hoping for, when Hick and Lewis were out in Ambrose's first over. And so it went on. We were bowled out for 355, a real waste of our brilliant start and a total which we felt wasn't enough on a pretty blameless wicket. Then we had what you might call an interesting little 45 minutes before lunch. I bowled well without luck, before we had an incident involving Phil Tufnell and an appeal for a run out.

Haynes had hit a straight four, Tufnell chased after it and just as he got to the big white wall at one end of the Kensington Oval, he tried to flick the ball back with his boot. He thought he'd succeeded in flicking it back before it touched the wall, so he picked it up and threw it in while the two batsmen, Haynes and Richie Richardson, were just talking in the middle of the wicket because they were sure the ball had gone for four. It went to Jack Russell and Tufnell was screaming at him, 'Run him out, run him out.' Jack took the bails off and appealed, and the poor umpires, Darrell Hair and Lloyd Barker, didn't know what to do.

By now Atherton and Haynes had got involved and had an exchange of words which went something like Dessie saying, 'This is my island,' and Athers saying, 'Yes, and we could blow it out of the ocean if we wanted to.' So there was a bit of ill feeling around for a while before lunch and we hadn't had the better of the session.

I remember thinking to myself at lunch, 'Things have got to change for the better; it can't carry on like this,' because I was having so little luck. And things did improve. My first wicket owed much to the captain. He asked me if I wanted a third slip and I said, 'Well, OK then.' The very next over, Richardson edged the ball there, to Athers himself, and I had got the break I needed. It would have gone through for four if Mike hadn't said that. Keith Arthurton went in the same over, caught behind by Jack, and I felt good.

I went off for a while soon after that. Sometimes you use the rules to your advantage. You're allowed to go off for

14 minutes and bowl as soon as you return, and you can use that time to have a rest and change your clothes, making sure you come out feeling a bit more refreshed. While I was off, Nasser Hussain, the substitute fielder, took a catch that I might not have done – diving at cover – to get rid of Lara off Lewis. I wrote in my diary, 'I might not have made it look so easy!' And then, when I returned after tea, I enjoyed one of those sessions when everything goes right. I moved to the far end, got close to the stumps and moved the ball away. They invariably nicked it and we caught most of the chances that came our way. It turned out to be a magnificent episode in my life.

Things were going my way and the cheering of the crowd was brilliant. I think it was a more special performance for me than those at Jamaica, Melbourne and The Oval simply because of the level of support we had on an away ground. In Jamaica, my wickets came instantly but almost too instantly, because it all happened in five overs. Nothing was quite as enjoyable as this. I felt confident enough to use the crease and had six wickets by the close, even though Chanderpaul was dropped, in a West Indies total of 188 for seven. My figures of six for 47 at that stage were career-best ones for me. But only until the morning.

Desmond Haynes, Jimmy Adams, Junior Murray and Winston Benjamin all fell to me, and that Lewis wicket while I was off the field was the only one not to fall to me that day. I also felt pretty strong at the close, so I concluded that I was getting fitter. We went out to a beach club run by a friend of Robin Smith's and had roast beef and Yorkshire pudding for our dinner – the first time I had tasted that for a while.

Day three

We let them off the hook, really, by letting them get to 304, just 51 behind us, with Chanderpaul, Ambrose and Kenny Benjamin all getting runs. Even Walsh chipped in with 13. I felt good for my first three or four overs but then it hit me. Mentally I was OK, but my legs were not doing what I wanted them to do – the previous day had obviously taken more out of me than I thought. Still, Ambrose was my seventh victim and then Walsh became my eighth as I finished with eight for 75. I didn't realise how many records those figures had broken at first. My concern was that our lead was not nearly as big as it should have been. It turned out that my return was the best by an England bowler against the West Indies and the best for England since Bob Willis took eight for 43 against Australia in the famous Headingley win of 1981.

We lost early wickets in our second innings but Stewart and Hick were superb, taking us to 171 for three at the close. Smith had another disappointing time. He had been struggling for much of the tour and said before this match that if he was going to go down, at least it would be with all guns blazing. But what happened? He was LBW to Kenny Benjamin without offering a stroke. We had a lead in excess of 220 and were feeling good about our position, but we felt we needed at least another 150 to be confident, on what was still a good batting track.

I had a meal at Pisces, a gorgeous little restaurant, with Denise to celebrate my eight-wicket haul and relax ahead of the rest day. I was much in demand after my 'eight-for' and did a lot of interviews around the pool on the rest day. I enjoy that sort of thing, particularly after

I've done well. In an England dressing-room, attitudes to the press vary, but most players seem 'anti' and won't be too co-operative with them. My view is different: by talking to reporters, maybe you can explain why things happen like they do in games and give them a better understanding of it all. You can also use the media to give yourself a good profile if you are clever about it. I certainly have no complaints about the coverage I've received in my career so far. I'm happy to answer the press questions, and it can also help promote the game if you make yourself available to them. Some players say they don't read the papers even if they do well, but I'd say they're liars! Everybody likes reading nice things about themselves and enjoys being in the headlines.

It's not an ego thing, it's just nice to be appreciated at times and after a while you accept that it's part of the job. I was very proud of my figures. At lots of grounds there are honours boards for occasions like this, and your name goes on it if you score a hundred or take a five-for. Unfortunately, there wasn't one at Bridgetown, but I'm on the one in the home dressing-room at Lord's twice, and I know that my name will be up there as long as Lord's is around, so that's a nice feeling.

My performance in Barbados is something I look back on with enormous pride. It's difficult to really appreciate now quite what the atmosphere was like during that match. I recently went back there on holiday and I took my parents to the Kensington Oval to have a look around. We stood in the middle and I tried to think back, but it was hard to picture it when you were standing in an empty ground. I just remember that, at the time, it was an amazing thrill.

Day four

Stewart and Thorpe smashed the West Indies all round the place in the afternoon session, the first time we'd really got on top of their bowling during the whole series. They really struggled to contain us and we'd gained the momentum by playing some good cricket. Their bowlers kept running in hard. They certainly weren't just going through the motions or anything like that, we were just better than them on the day. When Hick was out for a good 59, Alec just carried on, reaching his second hundred of the match, which was amazing. And once again, someone had stolen my glory and pipped me for the Man of the Match award!

Alec made his debut in our win in Jamaica in 1990 and has played pretty consistently for England ever since. He made his debut fairly late on for a class player, when he was approaching his 27th birthday, but he had always been an impressive county player and I suppose the rebel tour gave him his chance to come to the fore. He had played consistently well for Surrey and deserved his chance when it came his way. He had a few problems while he was becoming established and there were a few things said about his dad, Micky, being the manager. But I never thought that did him any favours at all. You would never have guessed that they were father and son when they were working together, and it was never something the other players talked about. It would have been easy to gossip about them, but it just never happened, and you have to take your hat off to the pair of them because they never allowed it to.

Alec has always been the model professional and perfectionist. He is meticulous in his preparation and the way he dresses, probably even more so since he's played international cricket. He's the Alan Shearer of our sport, Mr

Clean, Mr Nice. He looks good and does things right. You never see him unshaven or untidy. He's a bit of a tart in some ways. Sharing a hotel room with him can be a nightmare. You never have any room in the bathroom because it's always full of his vitamin tablets and skin lotions.

He is certainly a hard cricketer and doesn't let on about his true feelings at times. He can try it on, very much in the Surrey way – annoying to play against but great to have on your side. I've enjoyed Alec's company and he has worked hard to become a very good Test player. When he gets it right, he's capable of taking any side apart and can dominate proceedings. And as his career has gone on and he's gained more confidence, he's become better and better in his range of shots. Maybe he should have scored a few more centuries, but he's got a record to be proud of and is a survivor, too. Like so many good players, his career has been under threat at times but he's come through them.

Alec only got back into the side in 1996 when Nick Knight was injured, but then he made the most of it and scored more Test runs that year than anyone else in the world. That shows that even when the selectors write people off, there are those who will keep on coming back and proving the buggers wrong. I like to think I'm in that category, too.

Stewie is not a bad keeper, either. He has never let England down in that role. He first kept for England in a Test in Adelaide, when the selectors wanted to play an extra bowler in case I broke down with my hip injury, and he has done it often and well since. We have forever been in search of the new Ian Botham, but Alec is the closest we've had to a genuine Test all-rounder. He's used that situation to his advantage at times, wanting to keep when he hasn't been in the best form with the bat and not wanting to do it when he's been scoring runs, but it has also worked against him and he's been prepared to compromise part of his game for the team's cause. He shows immense powers of concentration and fitness, too, when he keeps and opens the batting in the same match.

On this occasion, Alec reached 143 before he was bowled by Walsh to add to his 118, and with Thorpe contributing 84, we were able to declare and set them 446 to win, 40 more than had ever been made to win a Test. We took two of their wickets before the close, too, but Brian Lara was still in residence and we had plenty of work left to do.

Day five

It got a bit tense at times and the game went into the final afternoon, but in the end we pulled off a remarkable victory by 208 runs. We had arrived in Barbados, what people said was the impregnable home of West Indian cricket, when we were close to rock-bottom after the Trinidad debacle and that terrible tour match in Grenada. West Indies had won their last 12 Tests on this ground, but we became the first visiting side to triumph here since RES Wyatt's England team 59 years earlier, and only the second team ever.

It wasn't my day at all with the ball and quite a few of their players got themselves in, but Andy Caddick was our main wicket-taker, claiming five for 63, and only Lara, with 64, held us up for any real length of time. Ambrose was the last man out, bowled by Lewis, and was so annoyed at his team's defeat that, pride surfacing again, he smashed the stumps with his bat, an indiscretion that cost him £1,000.

Not many people, however, noticed what Curtly was doing because the pitch was immediately full of invading England fans. But I can still remember short leg moving in to collect a souvenir stump only to be nearly cleaned up by Ambrose slogging it out of the ground. I managed to get one, which has been signed by the England team and, along with the ball I took eight wickets with, makes a very nice memento.

It was great to celebrate with those same supporters afterwards. We went out of the dressing-room to talk to them; most of us had friends and family there, but there were around 8,000 who had spent a lot of money to come and watch us. Hearing them say we had made their holiday was a big thrill, and we wouldn't have had to buy a drink all night if we had been able to stay in Bridgetown. As it was, we had to make a rapid departure.

The aftermath

When we should have been savouring one of the most unlikely and most satisfying of Test wins, we found ourselves hanging around at the airport in Barbados for our flight that night to Antigua for the final Test. It was quite an anti-climax. We had all agreed between ourselves that as soon as we reached Antigua we would meet up in Miller's bar along the beach from our hotel, but our team celebration never really happened.

The families were with us, which, for Denise and me, meant making sure Alex had a cot, a fridge and his bottles before I could go out, so I never made it to the bar. A lot of the other guys were in the same boat and, consequently, only about six of our number got there in the end. It was a shame, because enjoying the winning moment as a team is

(*Left*) A broken finger during a warm-up game in Barbados meant that I was on the sidelines at the beginning of the Test series to the West Indies in 1994 – having battled back into the England set-up, it was the last thing I needed. (*Ben Radford/Allsport*)

(*Below, left*) Jack Russell prepares to face the West Indian pace attack in the first Test at Jamaica.

(*Below, right*) Alan Igglesden revels in the luxurious lifestyle on tour with England in Guyana, with a board to support his bed. (both *Angus Fraser*)

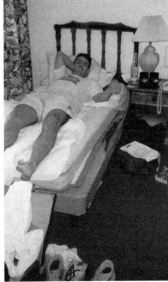

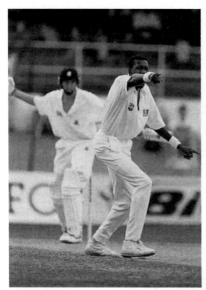

Curtly Ambrose traps Mike Atherton first ball in the second innings in Trinidad – it was the start of an awesome spell of fast bowling from him and Courtney Walsh. (*Ben Radford/Allsport*)

(*Below*) Celebrating with Alec Stewart after England's victory in the fourth Test in Barbados. He had scored a century in each innings, while I had taken eight for 75 – then the best figures ever for an Englishman against the West Indies, though I was to improve on them in 1998. (*Ben Radford/Allsport*)

Darren Gough's career really took off during the Ashes series of 1994–95. Here he celebrates taking the wicket of Steve Waugh at Sydney; Waugh is always such a thorn in our side. (*Graham Chadwick/Allsport*)

Graeme Hick is furious, and Graham Thorpe concerned, at England's declaration with him on 98 not out. Atherton's decision soured the atmosphere in the changing room. (*Patrick Eagar*)

Having not been part of the original tour party, I was delighted to prove Ray Illingworth wrong by taking five wickets in the second innings when I was called up to play in Sydney. Mark Waugh is my victim. (*Patrick Eagar*)

Mike Gatting, my Middlesex team-mate, silenced many of his critics with his 117 at Adelaide in the fourth Test. (*Patrick Eagar*)

important. When he took over, Mike Atherton tried to make sure that whenever we have won, we stayed together for an extra night in whatever hotel we are in, and I think that's right. We haven't won too many games, so it's vital for team spirit that you make the most of them when they come along.

Yet so often the system makes that difficult. After we beat the West Indies at Lord's in 1995, when Dominic Cork made such an impact on his debut, we all had to go straight off to NatWest Trophy first round matches. For Cork that meant a trip up to deepest Cambridgeshire so soon after doing so well, and for me it was even worse – two hours after defeating the West Indies, I was on the road to St Austell to face Cornwall the next day, a journey that involved spending six hours on a coach. That may be changed in the near future, and let's hope it is.

We had a couple of days off before the Antigua Test, a time when we were supposed to be reflecting on our win in Barbados and unwinding with our families. But we were to be rudely awoken. I distinctly remember sitting on our verandah with Denise and Alex, having a drink, when I was surrounded by about 15 press men. They wanted a reaction to the news from back home that Ray Illingworth, our new chairman of selectors, had suggested I wasn't fit enough for regular international cricket. I didn't know what to say.

I had just taken eight wickets in an innings during a famous England victory. I was perfectly happy with the way I was bowling and I was looking forward to playing in the last Test. Now it seemed our new man in charge wanted me to pull out of the game, and it was an early and immediate introduction to the chairman's fondness for speaking his mind to the press rather than to the individual concerned. Illingworth had pipped MJK Smith for the chairman's job and, as usual when things weren't going too well, there had been an inquest into what, at least before Barbados, was going wrong.

This was the first move towards England appointing a supremo, a man accountable for all the decisions. It was a principle I was in agreement with, but it was a question of getting the right person. I still don't know the full story as to why Illingworth's comments about me and other England players became public at a time when we should have been congratulating ourselves on a Test well won.

I believe he made them at a sports writers' lunch and perhaps he was naïve in thinking they would not get reported. But then again, he had spent enough time working in the media to be aware of how these things work. Maybe he thought his comments were off the record; maybe they were taken out of context. But they were always going to filter through to us and it wasn't the sort of thing we expected or wanted to hear from him, especially so soon after Barbados.

When it had first become clear that Illy had a chance of taking over the top job, there had been mutterings that exactly this sort of thing might happen. He had never been shy of criticising players in his *Daily Express* columns and we just hoped that he would curb his outspoken nature while he was working with us. Not a chance.

I was hurt. I had bowled almost 46 overs in Barbados, and if you throw yourself into every one of them like I do, then you are bound to look tired. You *should* be tired at the end of it, or you are not giving your all. But myself and Robin Smith, we discovered that day, were clearly not among the new chairman's favourites, and it was something that was to affect both our careers.

Poor Robin was receiving stick from another direction, too, in the build-up to Antigua. Keith Fletcher, during a press conference, suggested that Robin's business interests were interfering with his cricket – an unusual course of action for Keith to take, because he normally backed his players to the hilt. I can only imagine Fletch had become very frustrated for him to say that, and maybe there was something in it because at that time, Robin was a very busy man. But Robin wasn't happy and confronted Keith about it.

Perhaps players can be a bit sensitive to things like this; maybe they need saying at times. You should try not to get too emotional and fly off the handle every time you receive criticism, because sometimes it's what you need. A quiet word here and there is enough for some, but not others, and whether Robin's business interests were the cause of his bad form or not, he undoubtedly turned things around in the last Test with a big hundred. There was a famous line, after Keith and Robin had made their peace, when the manager urged Robin to go and get a big score. 'I'll get a hundred,' Robin promised. 'That's not enough,' said Fletcher. Robin scored 175.

So our relaxing couple of days had definitely gone out of the window and everything was going off again. But the Test at the St John's Recreation Ground would soon take our minds off things.

It's not usually good for the game when one side gets close to 600 and then the other matches it and there is barely time for another innings. The fifth Test in Antigua came into that category, but it was a game that will go down in history because of the contribution of Brian Charles Lara. We were on the receiving end of the highest individual score in Test history.

Richie Richardson wasn't playing in the match, so Courtney Walsh took over and immediately put an end to the previous dithering by winning the toss and saying, 'We'll bat.' I thought, 'There's a typical bowler. No p****** about. Now he can go and put his feet up!' The pitch looked flat, but we actually had a good start and got rid of Phil Simmons and Stuart Williams early. It raised our expectations, but we were soon brought back down to earth and the match became very hard work.

I actually felt I had bowled pretty well and got through 23 overs in the day, but I was tired by the end of it simply because there was no way past Lara's bat. It was the same after the second and the third days, too, as he just went on and on. It was an absolutely chanceless innings as he progressed to 164 by the end of the first day, 320 by the close on day two and then went on to better Sir Garfield Sobers's previous best of 365 by 10 runs before Caddick had him caught behind. Lara never slogged, went at the same tempo throughout and displayed incredible concentration. After each 50 he just raised his bat and carried on, and he didn't put a foot wrong until after he went past 300. Then I beat him a couple of times, went down the wicket and said, 'I don't suppose I can call you a lucky bastard when you've got 300 on the board.' He just smiled at me and carried on.

We were always aware, from an early stage, that he was going for the record and that the West Indies were going to give him the chance to get it. A score of 375 out of 593 for five declared is amazing, particularly on an outfield that was on the slow side. Lara is the best batsman I've bowled at, no question. People like Border and Richards were great, but even they were a little more limited in what they were capable of doing than he was.

Lara has such a range of shots that he can make you look stupid. Having such a good eye, he can score freely and gets away with most indiscretions on the strength of it. The goal was there for him that day and he just played and played and played until he reached it. The big moment came when he pulled Lewis for four, and some amazing scenes followed immediately afterwards. We weren't aware of what was going to happen, but the ground was suddenly full of people and Sobers was on his way out to the middle.

We all congregated in the middle because we knew the ground would take at least 10 minutes to clear and just watched while Lara kissed the ground and hugged Sobers. I thought it was a bit too much to set up a scene like that. We said to each other, 'I thought you just raised your bat when you reached a landmark.' Darrell Hair was the umpire and we asked him if the time lost would be taken into account when our over-rate was calculated. He said, 'How much time do you want?'

By this time, there were hundreds of people on the outfield and the umpires were desperately trying to keep them off the wicket because we still had to bat on it. They all moved away, but there was one bloke walking up and down the pitch looking to see if there was any damage to it and Hair went up to him and pushed him out of the way, telling him to p*** off. Then he discovered it was actually the groundsman inspecting his beloved wicket.

The outfield was eventually cleared and we got ready to resume, but then somebody said, 'Where's the ball?' We all went back to our marks, and square leg went trotting over to the boundary to discover the ball nestling by a board in exactly the place where it came to rest after Lara's pull. Nobody had noticed it there and picked it up. It would have made a great souvenir for a spectator, but it became a souvenir for Lara because, later, I got it off the umpires and had it signed by the five members of our attack – myself, Caddick, Tufnell, Lewis and Hick – before presenting it to the record-breaker. He was delighted to receive it, although with hindsight, I wish I'd kept it for my benefit. It would have raised a few bob. Lara actually swapped a tracksuit with me after the series and signed it, but I didn't auction that one. I've kept it because it's a nice reminder of being part of a history-making innings.

Lara was a very charming man then, but he seems to have changed a bit over the last couple of years. He seems to have become shorter with people. At that time I got on very well with him, and we would have a couple of drinks and generally socialise and enjoy each other's company. I haven't seen him enough to call him a friend, but he was an opposing player I got on well with. Then, when we played Warwickshire the following summer soon after Lara had broken the other big record by scoring 501 against Durham, the highest first-class innings, things seemed to be different. I would ask him if he wanted to come for a drink at the tavern, but at the end of play, his agent would be waiting for him and he would be off doing all sorts of things.

It's difficult to put yourself in his position because no one in cricket has been as big as him before. So what must it be like? It's impossible for the rest of us to tell, but I do know he's under a lot of pressure to perform. He also forever has people wanting a piece of his time and clearly has an agent running his life to no small degree. I would like to see him being allowed to enjoy himself and do what he wants. Perhaps he has got a bit too outspoken and demanding, because he must fancy himself after what he's achieved, but I remember him, in 1994, as a bloody nice lad and I would hate to think of him being spoilt by it all. It will be interesting to see how his career develops.

Since the highs of 1994 he hasn't scored quite the same quantity of runs, but it was always going to be a hard act to follow. Glenn McGrath got him out a few times when the Aussies last played them by tucking him up, a simple plan which has often been used to good effect against top-quality strokemakers. Lara still tries to be dominant, so I think we bowlers will be looking at McGrath's example and trying similar methods. I think Lara feels he can do what he wants on the field, but he might have to accept that opposing players are a bit better than he gives them credit for.

We did well when we batted after the Lara show – a lot of people were expecting us to capitulate in the face of such a big score. Antigua is a brilliant place to play cricket, because of the music and the atmosphere. Every time a boundary is hit or a wicket is taken, the little stand next to the pavilion is like a disco, with everybody dancing and a character called Gravy gyrating and hanging off the stand. When we had a rain-break during the fifth Test, the whole place was just like a club and we couldn't hear ourselves think above the noise. It was almost a disappointment when the game started again, because it was such good fun.

It can be horrible, as a bowler, to walk off after your side has gone for such a big score and then watch your openers face the first few overs. You wonder if the wicket is really as flat as it seemed when you were bowling on it, and you fear what the opposition might do. How often have we heard commentators say 'and now we'll get a true reflection of what's in the surface when the West Indies bowlers perform on it'? You think it's flat and then suddenly Ambrose gets the ball whizzing past a batsman's nose. Meanwhile, the batsmen waiting to go in say, 'What's wrong with our bowlers? That didn't happen when we were out there.' Thankfully, there was none of that this time. After about six overs I realised it was flat for them, too, so I was hugely relieved and watched contentedly as Atherton and Robin Smith got centuries and we batted ourselves to a creditable draw. I was out for nought, so I could say I formed half of the biggest differential in Test cricket scores – Fraser 0 and Lara 375!

We were told this was a new dawn with a young side and that we were going to stick with this party for a while, even though we'd lost the series 3–1. We had played some good cricket, particularly in the last two Tests, and had been in the box seat for much of the Trinidad match, too. Yes, we had lost the first two games heavily, but there were some good points to look back on and a feeling that things would not come right overnight and we must give it a bit of time.

Then we came back to be greeted by an absolute zoo at the airport, with photographers pushing and shoving and reporters trying to get a reaction to what Illingworth had said about us. I came through with Alex and he was in the middle of this scrum, so I ended up shoving a couple of photographers out of the way to make room for my son. I then got grilled over Illingworth questioning my fitness and

I had a bit of a go back at him, saying that as far as I was concerned there were no problems with my physical condition and that I had bowled well on tour. I also said that if the chairman had anything to say about my fitness, he should say it to me, rather than talk to the papers. I suppose it could be argued that I was getting into a bit of a slanging match, but I was quite annoyed. There was a lot more, however, to come from Mr Illingworth. I said goodbye to the lads, not knowing how many of them I would be seeing on England duty that summer, as I prepared to go straight back into an English season.

England to the West Indies 1993–94

First Test
Sabina Park, Kingston, Jamaica, 19, 20, 21, 23, 24 February
England 234 (A.J.Stewart 70, M.A.Atherton 55, K.C.G.Benjamin 6 for 66)
and 267 (G.A.Hick 96)
West Indies 407 (K.L.T.Arthurton 126, J.C.Adams 95 not out, B.C.Lara 83)
and 95 for 2
Result: West Indies won by 8 wickets.

Second Test
Bourda, Georgetown, Guyana, 17, 18, 19, 20, 22 March
England 322 (M.A.Atherton 144, R.A.Smith 84) and 190 (A.J.Stewart 79)
West Indies 556 (B.C.Lara 167, J.C.Adams 137, D.L.Haynes 63,
S.Chanderpaul 62)
Result: West Indies won by an innings and 44 runs.

Third Test
Queen's Park Oval, Port-of-Spain, Trinidad, 25, 26, 27, 29, 30 March
West Indies 252 (R.B.Richardson 63) and 269 (S.Chanderpaul 50,
A.R.Caddick 6 for 65)
England 328 (G.P.Thorpe 86, C.E.L.Ambrose 5 for 60) and 46
(C.E.L.Ambrose 6 for 24)
Result: West Indies won by 147 runs.

Fourth Test
Kensington Oval, Bridgetown, Barbados, 8, 9, 10, 12, 13 April
England 355 (A.J.Stewart 118, M.A.Atherton 85) and 394 for 7 dec
(A.J.Stewart 143, G.P.Thorpe 84, G.A.Hick 59, C.A.Walsh 5 for 94)
West Indies 304 (S.Chanderpaul 77, A.R.C.Fraser 8 for 75) and 237
(B.C.Lara 64, K.L.T.Arthurton 52, A.R.Caddick 5 for 63)
Result: England won by 208 runs.

Fifth Test
Recreation Ground, St John's, Antigua, 16, 17, 18, 20, 21 April
West Indies 593 for 5 dec (B.C.Lara 375, S.Chanderpaul 75 not out,
J.C.Adams 59) and 43 for 0
England 593 (R.A.Smith 175, M.A.Atherton 135, C.C.Lewis 75 not out,
R.C.Russell 62)
Result: Match drawn.

Angus Fraser's tour (2nd, 3rd, 4th and 5th Tests):
Batting: 6 innings, 3 not out, high score 8 NO, runs 11, average 3.66.
Bowling: 168.5 overs, 39 maidens, 443 runs, 16 wickets, average 27.68, best
8–75.

england in australia 1994-95

The background

We arrived back in England from the West Indies on 22 April, and as Middlesex had won the championship in 1993, they were already back in action facing England A in the season's opening match. I had one day off before heading for Lord's and was playing again by the 26th. No rest for the wicked.

Yet I felt fresh and enthusiastic. I was playing for my county again and it felt different, a change being almost as good as a rest in this case. I was bowling on responsive pitches and a lot of people said that I seemed to be enjoying my cricket more than I'd ever done. I think they were right. I had returned from injury and done well in the West Indies, and it was all like a bonus after what I had been through. Life was good.

But for some reason, I actually struggled throughout the 1994 domestic season. My best bowling in all cricket that year was three for 16, and even that was only getting the tail out. Wickets were hard to come by and my wicket tally for Middlesex went down, a trend that I have not been able to correct since. Ever since that time, even when I've bowled a lot better than I did in 1994, I haven't got the volume of wickets that I feel my bowling has deserved in county cricket. It's a mystery to me. I don't think I'm kidding myself. I think I'm bowling well, week in and week out, but I've been struggling like hell to reach 50 wickets a season, something I should do comfortably. Then I've looked at the averages and the scorecards and seen that such and such a bowler has taken 'six-for' in an innings, and I'm baffled why I can't do the same.

Anyway, my early-season enjoyment in 1994 soon came to an end when England faced New Zealand. Things just didn't go my way and, even though I only went for around two an over, I only took seven wickets in three games at about 40 apiece. We won the three-Test series 1–0, Darren Gough came onto the scene with a bang and there were a lot of plusses for English cricket. But the series was rapidly overshadowed by the second half of the Test summer.

South Africa's return to Lord's for their first Test in England since their reintroduction to the international scene was always going to be a big occasion. What it also became was a hammering for us and the game where our young captain became embroiled in the biggest controversy of the sporting year.

Mike Atherton could easily have lost his job after what became known as the 'dirt in the pocket' scandal, but the whole thing was taken out of all proportion and became far bigger than it ever should have done. The thing is, if Mike had rubbed sawdust on the ball, it would have been OK, but as it was dry earth and he didn't appear to be applying it openly, then the whole world went mad. They called him a cheat. But what's the difference between sawdust and dust? Just judging by his actions, I suppose, people thought Mike was being mischievous – and on TV it certainly looked that way – but the reaction was incredible. I didn't know what was going on at the time. I was aware we were trying to get reverse swing, so I was trying to keep the ball as dry as I could, but I wasn't aware until that evening of Mike having done anything with the ball.

Then the following day, after we were bowled out for double figures to lose convincingly, we had the TV on in the dressing-room and all of a sudden a press conference came on featuring Mike. We all thought it was the BBC 'feed' – which we can carry on watching even if they go over to the news or the racing – and had no idea the whole thing was going out live. Only when it was over and they went back to the presenter did it dawn on us that the authorities had put Mike up there in front of everybody and left him to get on with it. To put your captain in that situation is ridiculous; talk about throwing him to the lions. We all just felt so sorry for the bloke.

All right, Ray Illingworth says he saved Mike's job that night – and didn't let him forget it for God knows how long – but to put him in that position was terrible. I went out with Atherton that night in Hampstead and he didn't know what to do. His pride was wounded and he wasn't sure if he should quit or not. I said to him, 'Let them make the decision.' I don't know if it had any effect on him, but thankfully, he stayed.

I got five wickets in that match but didn't bowl well in the next game at Headingley and got left out at The Oval, a game which we won dramatically after Devon Malcolm took nine wickets in the South Africans' second innings. When you get dropped, the temptation is to compare yourself with the players they've picked ahead of you, but on this occasion I accepted the decision and thought: 'Fair enough. I haven't set the world alight this summer.' I was even slightly relieved that the pressure was off me for a while. A lot of players in the Middlesex dressing-room seemed shocked that I'd been dropped, but I wasn't sure if they were just being nice to me.

My body was feeling tired. Maybe I was trying too hard. I had been playing virtually non-stop for 18 months and I think every player needs a rest after a while. The effort of throwing yourself at the game every day catches up with you. Maybe the workload knocks the edge off your game but you don't admit that to yourself or others at the time.

I had tried to make my relationship with Illingworth work. It was all a bit stand-offish at first, but we had been getting on all right. By this time, though, he had a couple of sidekicks, Brian Bolus and Fred Titmus, involved, and I quickly realised where I stood with Bolus. Geoff Boycott was getting on my case a bit during the Old Trafford Test against New Zealand, saying I wasn't doing enough with the ball, and Bolus apparently was echoing this in the dressing-room while we were on the field. I walked past him at tea and he said, 'Well bowled, fella.' Then I went into the dressing-room and someone I was close to, who was in there, told me Bolus had been less complimentary about me. I thought, 'What's going on?'

Devon bowled magnificently at The Oval and Joey Benjamin, who had come in ahead of me for his debut, had a good game, too. It had ended up being a reasonable summer for us. There had been a steady influx of Yorkshire players in the side – I wonder why? – and I had been left out at The Oval, but the thought of missing out on a tour place didn't enter my head.

I was picked for the one-dayers, which finished the season, and only started to get an uneasy feeling because of the way Mike was talking. He didn't say anything directly, but from his attitude towards me I got the impression that I might be under a bit of pressure for my Australian place. It made me feel a bit uncomfortable and the night before the tour party was announced, I found myself sitting at home, almost waiting for the phone to ring giving me bad news. But it never did. I didn't hear anything, so I went to bed assuming I was in.

Even then I thought the phone might ring very late, or early the following morning, but it didn't, so I turned on Sky TV's coverage of the tour announcements anticipating good news. The party was read out and they went straight from DeFreitas to Gatting, which sent my mind into turmoil. I found myself going through the alphabet in my mind, desperately hoping I had somehow got it wrong and that F came after G. Then I heard the name McCague and it hit me that I wasn't there. I just turned to Denise and said, 'I'm not going.' She said, 'You must be.' We were in a state of absolute shock and I found myself in tears.

Illingworth, when talking about this in his subsequent book *One-Man Committee*, said that no one had a right to play for England, and I agree with that. It's just that if you want players to go out there and be fully committed, to die for you, then you must treat them with respect and give them the courtesy of a call when they're not selected, particularly if they are an established part of the squad.

I thought it was disgraceful that no one, including Michael Atherton, one of my best friends in the game, had rung me before the announcement to let me know that I wouldn't be going. This was not the equivalent of one of your mates not turning up for a drink down the pub.

Representing England is the ultimate and should be treated as such. By not letting me know, they had cheapened that. All right, I'd have still been desperately upset about not going even if I'd been told in advance, but I would have found it easier to take and the management wouldn't have left themselves open to criticism that way.

Both Atherton and Keith Fletcher eventually rang me, but not until the Saturday morning, when the decision had been made on the Thursday night. They said they wanted to apologise and that they had both done as much as they could to get me on the tour, but that the other three selectors had gone for Martin McCague of Kent. I was almost in tears on the phone to both of them. They said that they hadn't rung earlier because the meeting ended late and the announcement was early the next morning, but it didn't really wash. They did both seem genuinely upset that I wasn't going, though, which was a consolation of sorts.

Before that, I had received another phone call, this time from David Norrie of the *News of the World*, asking me if I wanted to say anything in that week's paper about my omission. The papers had been full of me not going, so I thought I would do it to give my side of the story. I suppose in some ways I did the article for the money, but it was mainly to vent my frustrations. All of a sudden, around £30,000 that I'd bargained on earning for my winter's work had gone out of the window, and I felt I had to try to get it back somehow. My *News of the World* fee was £2,000, so that was a start.

I wasn't sure if it was the right thing to do, but I did it. Then the next day I went and played for my club side Stanmore, surrounding myself with good friends at a time of crisis, and had a great day with them. It was the last day of the Middlesex County League season and we were playing Richmond. It rained all day but we played on because Richmond had a chance of winning the league. We stopped them doing that and then had a great night in the bar, which ended up with me getting totally drunk and having a sing-song to drown my sorrows.

Norrie had earlier sent the article through to me for checking and my eyes went straight away to the word 'gutless', a term I hadn't used. I had actually said that it was easy to phone someone up after the tour party had been announced, but that it would have shown guts to do it beforehand. I wanted 'gutless' taken out because I could see the headline coming, but they didn't change it and sure enough, the next day, the headline screamed 'You're gutless' out of the page at me, which was pretty strong. But I was very upset, so I wasn't too worried about that.

The question then was, 'What do I do now?' It was quickly answered for me when I got a call from a friend in Sydney asking if I wanted to play grade cricket for Western Suburbs. I thought, 'Why not?' It would mean Denise and Alex could come out for the whole winter to a place which ranks, after London, as my second favourite city. Then I got a letter from the TCCB saying I was on stand-by and to keep fit. I told them I was going to Australia, which they felt was even better, so the blow was beginning to be eased. Until, that is, I got a phone call from Illingworth.

He told me that my stand-by fee was being reduced from £5,000 to £4,000 because my article in the *News of the World* was unacceptable. I was being fined and warned about my future conduct. He then said the matter was now closed and that I would start the following summer with a clean sheet. He also said he liked me and my approach to the game, but that they had picked a side for Australia that they thought was the best for the job. I told him I intended to prove him wrong and he added that he would be happy if I did. In a way, it was good that I'd finally spoken to him about it – and I'd heard that there was even a chance I would be thrown off stand-by duty because of the article, so perhaps the £1,000 fine wasn't too bad. But I couldn't help coming off the phone feeling as if I'd been bullied and threatened.

I think Mike might have had a word on my behalf when the possibility of them throwing me out completely had been raised, along the lines of, 'He's had one kick in the teeth, don't kick him again.' When he told me about it, I said to him: 'Athers, if they're prepared to throw me off stand-by duty just for having my say, then they can stick it. I don't want to play in a set-up where players are treated like that. If you can't have the right of reply over a decision that's been made, then why bother?' He told me not to be silly and that I was letting my emotions run away with me. But I still feel that way today.

After that, I just got on with my winter. I played in an ill-fated floodlit venture at The Oval before spending a week in India as a guest player, along with Desmond Haynes, in a one-day tournament in Bangalore. It was at a time when there was a scare over the plague in India, and going there also meant that I would have to miss Ricky Ellcock's wedding, which I felt bad about. But I was being well paid for going to India and I had to think of making my money up, so I went. The plague scare certainly didn't bother me and I think that Dessie and me going made the West Indies realise that it was safe to carry on with their planned tour there, so we might have done the Indian Board a financial favour, too.

The build-up

We left for Australia on 18 October. Grade cricket is not a great payer but it's good cricket, good fun and gives you a chance to spend the winter with your family in a lovely place. I worked on my fitness because I was on stand-by for the England tour, did some coaching in schools and enjoyed my time with the family. Then, just as we were getting settled and had made a commitment on a flat of our own in Burwood, I received a phone call from MJK Smith, the England tour manager. He wanted me to get up to Brisbane, where the team were preparing for the first Test, as soon as possible because they had already experienced injury problems and wanted me to act as cover. I left straight away, leaving Denise and Alex in our new flat. Denise again had very mixed emotions. She was delighted for me that I was getting back in the fold, but it cannot have been too pleasant for her to spend her second night in our new flat alone with our 18-month-old son.

As soon as I arrived I had a meal with Mike Atherton, Keith Fletcher and Dave Roberts, the physio, and I gathered straight away that the team hadn't made the best of starts and quite a few things had been happening off the field. I got the impression that they felt a few players who they had picked were not what the selectors thought they were, and they seemed a bit depressed about the whole thing. I practised with the team, mainly covering for Devon who had chickenpox, but I couldn't see my involvement lasting for long. I wrote in my diary that: 'I was just feeling concerned that my hip was hurting me a bit when the phone rang and it was MJK Smith. As soon as I joined up with the team, I remembered what a different lifestyle this was. There were a lot of moans and groans among the players about silly little things, but I was so grateful to be there that my attitude was just to get on with it.' I had been on the outside, something I didn't like, and was struggling to show much sympathy for their problems. When you play for England, you get things completely out of proportion and it's only when you are back in the real world that you realise how trivial most of your 'problems' are.

Illingworth, who had not yet come out to Australia, had been sniping in the papers again, saying that I shouldn't have been called up. I also found out that Phil Tufnell had spent a night in a psychiatric hospital because he was having problems at home, a matter of enormous concern to the team. But when I saw Tuffers he seemed to be OK.

It was my first experience of MJK Smith as a tour manager and I found him refreshing and funny. He wasn't prepared, for instance, to run around after the players, as some managers will, performing their chores for them. If someone asked him to get some little thing for them, he would say, 'Get it yourself.' Then there was the time I went up to his room for something at 8.30am and he was sitting there drinking a can of beer. This was a man who didn't drink much at all and who would not have touched another drop that day, but it was one of his little quirks that endeared him to me.

I found my first net session with the team a real eye-opener. I wrote: 'It's embarrassing, really. When I ran up and bowled, I was better than anybody else here. They knew it, too. I feel they want me here.' I was soon, however, on my way back to Sydney when they decided that, for now, they could cope without me.

I was around just long enough for the first session of the Test, which started in the worst possible way when Michael Slater smashed Phil DeFreitas's first ball for four. You could almost hear our dressing-room groaning. It knocked the stuffing out of us right at the very start. The initiative had been grabbed by them immediately and by the time I left, less than two hours later, Australia were 87 without loss already. By the time my flight landed in Sydney, I saw that the score was already 280 for two and I thought, 'Jesus, what's gone on there?' The ball had apparently flown everywhere. It was 'help yourself' time.

I went to practice that night with Western Suburbs and later wrote: 'The blokes at Wests think I'm the unluckiest man in the world to have that lot picked in front of me.' It certainly didn't look as if we were going to blast them out, which was the idea before the tour. We ended up losing the first Test, crushingly, by 184 runs, but I was soon on my way to join up with the party again, this time for the duration of the tour. McCague had had to pull out with stress fractures to his shins, so I was called up in time for the two games against the Australian Academy. I was soon wondering what I had let myself in for.

We were heavily beaten by the Academy on both occasions, with me getting hit for two sixes to finish the first game and the second being even worse for us. It was terrible. We were dead. There was no atmosphere in the field and I wrote that 'some of the blokes just don't seem interested'. We were lower than any side I'd seen on tour before. I felt concerned for Mike Atherton, who was at his wits' end, and I was again annoyed when the bulk of the players just left the dressing-room straight away after the matches. I thought, 'How about sitting down and thinking about this?'

I went for a drink in the opposition dressing-room where Rod Marsh, who is in charge of the Academy, made the point that we were facing good cricketers, not some raw teenagers. That didn't stop Fletcher giving us a rollicking, and the whole party was quiet and subdued. Meanwhile, I had some stuff to sort out in Sydney. My parents were on their way out to help Denise, and things like reimbursement to Wests for my departure had to be fixed. We had furnished a flat which we now didn't need, so there were a lot of things to consider.

I had gone straight into the side – no worries about me being a replacement now – and I saw the new stand at Melbourne for the first time when we went there. It was amazing, holding 42,000, like putting the whole of Anfield football ground into one stand. We continued on our mainly disappointing journey, with injuries cropping up here, there and everywhere and people generally feeling sorry for themselves. There was no confidence nor conviction.

I was feeling fairly ineffective myself much of the time. I'd bowled well in grade cricket but being thrown into a match situation against good players on flat pitches was a different story.

I joined up with my family in Melbourne for Christmas and felt good in the nets, but I was left out of the second Test which started on Christmas Eve, with Christmas Day a rest day. The press show was good, with Illingworth being portrayed as God in a Yorkshire nativity play. Then there was the usual fancy-dress party and this time I went as Lurch from the Addams family while Denise was Morticia and Alex was a baby Gomez.

Back on the field the next day, the match started slipping away from us until we were eventually hammered again, with Shane Warne taking a hat-trick. The silence in the dressing-room while that was going on was broken by Phil Tufnell, who was the next man in after the hat-trick ball and who had got a duck in the first innings. Tuffers stood up, turned to the manager and said, '**** me, Fletch, I'm on a pair and a quadruple here!' He survived the quadruple ball but not his pair.

So we were 2–0 down and the Ashes were again slipping away. Illingworth had now arrived and was denying all responsibility for what had gone on before, and we were all at a really low ebb approaching the third Test at Sydney. I didn't think I'd be playing in that one. We'd been doing really badly, but for some reason I thought they would stick with the same people.

Third Test, Sydney Cricket Ground; 1–5 January 1995

Day one

Even on the first morning of the match, I didn't think I was playing. I had turned up, having been named in the squad, and Fletcher told me to have a bowl at the batsmen in the nets round the back, so I assumed I wasn't in the XI. Then, when I walked back to the middle for the team stretches, I began to realise that DeFreitas had a problem with his hamstring. Before I knew it, he had to pull out and I was in. It almost happened too quickly for me to get myself in the right frame of mind, but I was delighted. I was pleased that we batted, as it gave me time to settle and work on my confidence, which wasn't that high.

We had won the toss but were soon in familiar trouble at 20 for three, with Gooch, Hick and Thorpe all gone. Nerves by this time were really getting to me, but Atherton and Crawley started to go really well so I found a position out the back and stayed there with a few others, including Gooch. Eventually, I was told to pad up because I was on nightwatchman's duty, and as soon as I moved, wickets started to fall. Both John and Mike missed their centuries but had done really well in adding 174, and then I found myself in with half an hour to go. What should happen but I was immediately involved in a run out with Steve Rhodes, who had a miserable tour. I don't know whose fault it was, but when I realised what had happened I tried to run myself out because Steve is a better batsman than me. Steve Waugh, though, turned and threw it to the other end, where 'Bumpy' was stranded. I thought, 'I'll be in Illy's good books now, running out one of his little Yorkies.' It was the end for poor Rhodes. He thought that being run out by the nightwatchman just about put the lid on his tour and that things couldn't get any worse. Apparently, he drop-kicked his helmet across the dressing-room when he got back there. And we were in another bad position at the close on 198 for seven.

Day two

But things got better. This was the day that Darren Gough, to all intents and purposes, announced himself to the Test world, joining me at the crease and striking the ball superbly all round the park. He had bowled well before now, but the way he took Craig McDermott apart made a name for him as we put on 58 for the eighth wicket. I kept blocking and he kept hitting and it was great fun until he was out hooking McDermott to fine leg for 51. I encouraged Darren to keep on going for it. You have to, in that sort of situation. You have to have fun while the force is with you, and if I'd tried to tell him to play a different way, there's every chance he would have tried a different shot and had his pole knocked out of the ground.

Devon Malcolm came in and caught the mood and after three balls he was on 10. I, meanwhile, had reached nine by this stage because I was stonewalling it, so I thought it was time for me to try to open my shoulders, too. Devon just slapped it everywhere, hitting Warne for two big sixes as he raced to 29. I got out for 27, which disappointed me hugely because I only needed three more for my best in Test cricket, which, in this match at the SCG, would have meant my name flashing in lights on the scoreboard, an event which greeted each career best, however small.

The end came when Damien Fleming bowled me a short one and I tried to pull it and got a top edge into the air. But we had done well to get up to 309 after being 197 for seven and the three of us – Gough, Malcolm and Fraser – had all enjoyed ourselves hugely. We weren't out of the woods, but at least we had made ourselves a bit more competitive. It would take them a day and a bit to get past us even though the wicket was pretty flat, and we were delighted and relieved to post a respectable score after what had happened in Brisbane and Melbourne. The Aussies were only able to receive five overs before rain brought an end to the day.

Day three

It's amazing how the weather can change a game of cricket. All it needs is a bit of rain, a bit of moisture in the atmosphere and a day's play can be completely different. Now the luck that we hadn't had in previous games was with us. We turned up on the third morning when it was overcast and the wicket was still damp. We bowled a good line and length, the wicket did just enough to keep us interested and we had the Aussies 57 for six by lunch. Gough got three of them, Malcolm two and I got the wicket of Michael Bevan, who was caught at slip. Then, straight after lunch, I got rid of Shane Warne and Australia, incredibly, were 65 for eight, needing 110 to avoid the follow-on. We had them on the rack.

But Mike Atherton took me off and brought Devon back, thinking he would blast the last two out, and they managed to lift their total beyond the follow-on mark and up to 116. McDermott slogged his way to 21 while Mark Taylor, who was there from the start, was the ninth man to fall on 49. The follow-on had been avoided when a bouncer from Devon flew over Rhodes's head for four byes. Still, it had been a great effort from us and it was great for me to be back in Test cricket, with figures of two for 26 from 11 overs. When I was first called up from grade cricket and faced the Academy, it immediately struck me that there was a big difference in the game when you're representing your country. Then there was a bigger difference when we faced Queensland, and now there was a bigger difference still.

I can't actually say I was standing at the end of my run feeling good about things and full of confidence. I was pretty nervous and hesitant, which I'm not normally when I've got a ball in my hand. I was wondering how it would come out, because I hadn't done the amount of bowling to get me in the right frame of mind. Even after they were all out I was wondering if what I'd done was enough, but everybody seemed pleased enough. Gough got the last two wickets to finish with six for 49 to follow his 51, his first five-wicket haul in Test cricket. How he deserved it.

Darren was a figure the press and public loved. He was a chirpy, bouncy little character who fancied himself a bit and had the looks to go with it. He played with a smile on his face and people responded to that. They were looking for someone to brighten the English game up and he did that straight away. He can certainly bowl. Perhaps he has a disadvantage for a fast bowler in that he's quite small and that means, when the wickets are flat, that he might not be able to get that crucial extra bounce and could skid it onto the bat a bit. But he can be quick, swings the ball when he gets it right and has a big heart. Darren is a confident bloke who will always try things, perhaps sometimes trying too much without sticking to a stock ball he can rely on. But he was what England were looking for at this time. Because of the way he throws himself at the game, there is always the danger that he'll pick up injuries and he's had a few already, notably when his foot cracked during his run-up in a one-day match at Melbourne later on this tour. He's strong but he's quite heavily built and, tearing up, he can throw himself off his feet if he's not careful. He needs to play that way, though, to be fully effective. I suppose he could have a bit more control at times, but you wouldn't want that to come at the expense of his pace.

He also enjoys the adulation of the crowd, an early example of which we got then in Sydney when he took one of his six wickets. We all ran towards the stumps, as you do, to congregate and congratulate a bowler, but Darren ran straight through us, celebrating by almost doing a lap of honour with his arms outstretched. We were wondering what on earth he was doing. When he finally joined us, he was told in no uncertain terms that if he did that again we wouldn't be waiting for him because we weren't there to stand around and watch while he went mad. He's also someone you can take with a pinch of salt. For instance, if you tell Darren you've got a Rover GTi then he'll say he's got a GTi turbo. He's always got the best and that's the way he is, a deal here and a deal there. The consolation which has come from his injuries is that they have shown him how quickly it can all go wrong and how hard you must work to stay at the top.

He was built up very quickly as a 'star' on this tour but has subsequently had to put up with being out of the side. He has come through that well. It's something a lot of players have to go through and if you can be level-headed and not get carried away, then you'll be all the stronger for the experience. Some people do get carried away with it all when they first come into the England side. They can become a superstar and want this and want that. They then have to realise that cricket is the most important thing and that when that's right, everything else will fall into place. Darren should now be around for some time.

He was actually fed up that there wasn't an honours board at the SCG because he wanted to see his achievement on the wall for posterity. So he ended up chalking D Gough 6–49 on a noticeboard in the dressing-room area. I was reminded of that in the 1997 season when Glenn McGrath and Matthew Elliott posted notable performances at Lord's for Australia in the second Test. When I went back to Lord's the day after the match finished, I saw that someone had put tape across the honours board and put McGrath's and Elliott's names and achievements across them. I wondered if they had remembered what Gough had done in Sydney two years earlier?

So Australia avoided the follow-on and then, after losing Gooch, we battled really well in the second innings in the guise of Atherton and Hick. We finished on 90 for one, in a strong position to push for victory.

Day four

This was the first time that we had really got on top of their bowling in the series. Mike and Graeme were smashing it around and Australia were getting very defensive. The dressing-room was ecstatic. After Mike was out, Graham Thorpe joined Hick and smashed it around, too, and rarely had we known such riches! But, as if to stop us getting carried away, our mood was radically altered by a decision from our captain that he himself now admits was a mistake.

The atmosphere in the dressing-room was brilliant, but

then Atherton declared with Hick on 98 and there was an audible sigh as everyone immediately became deflated. It was like we were all thinking, 'You can't do that. You shouldn't have done that.' We were in a top position, but then we all walked onto the field with our heads down and even with some English supporters booing. I wrote in my diary: 'I could see Athers mulling it over and I think he did it to show who's boss. He can be stubborn at times. You do need to make unpopular decisions as captain, but this one was wrong.'

I could understand that things were getting tight and the captain wanted to bowl at them for 20 minutes before tea and then leave us four full sessions to win the match. But I think he got the timings wrong anyway. Hick, admittedly, was getting to his landmark slowly, but he wasn't getting much of the strike. Mike said that Graeme wasn't making enough of an effort to get there and that the game was more important. Again, I know what he means and yes, Hick had been a bit slow; yes, he had been told to get a move on. But I'm sorry, some things are more important than that, and this was a big innings for Graeme Hick.

I like Hicky a lot and have got on well with him since our first tour together. He's a nice, quiet lad who is meticulous in his approach. I know that some people, for various reasons, have not been too disappointed to see him struggling to do himself justice for England, and Graeme did set himself up a bit early in his career by playing up to his image as the Great Hope of English Cricket and bringing out a book called *My Early Years*. He was probably just advised badly at the time, agents encouraging him to cash in.

Now, having got to know him, how much he cares and the pride he takes in his cricket, I think he's a top man, and I was very upset to see him like this. Remember, too, that he had told me in the West Indies a year earlier that he would pay a million pounds for the extra four runs when he was on 96. He was that desperate to succeed, prove that he was good enough for the Test stage and worthy of the things that had been said about him. But he didn't get his century on that occasion, either.

It's not easy to pinpoint the reasons why he hasn't done as well as he should. Maybe it's a similar situation to Mark Ramprakash's: just because they have done extremely well in county cricket doesn't automatically mean they will be good enough for Tests. Some struggle with the stage, the spotlight, the attention, the crowd and the media. Some go into their shell, don't play their normal game and, because of that, they're not the same players. I've seen Graeme smash it around in one-day internationals and thought, 'That's the Hick I know,' but it hasn't been that way often enough in Test cricket.

Some say he can't play the short ball, but there have been a lot like that in Test cricket. He's a big man, and any big man finds it harder to get out of the way of the short stuff. And his courage? Well, I've not been aware of him wanting to get away from the hostile stuff. Maybe some can see a problem there, but all I see is a very committed cricketer and, really, he hasn't done as badly as some would have you believe. If you look at his record, it's not that bad – but with him, the expectations have been so high and the pressures much greater than most of us have had to tolerate. Anyway, it's not that easy out there in the middle. If it was, there would be hundreds of world-class cricketers knocking on the door. You've got to remember that there is a bowler trying just as hard at the other end.

When Hick walked in after that declaration, his thoughts on the subject were clear. He is normally mild but he threw his bat and gloves down and was obviously close to tears. I didn't know what to say, so I said nothing. Keith Fletcher went and sat next to him to say something, but Graeme just got up and walked away. When we fielded, he was at slip with Atherton but they didn't say a word to each other throughout the afternoon. I remember one occasion when there was an edge to third man and Graeme chased it to the boundary. He stopped it going for four and then threw back to Rhodes as hard as I've seen a cricket ball thrown in my life. There was real anger there that he had been deprived of a Test century because of a declaration. I go on more than anybody about batsmen being selfish and how it can affect a side, but I'd never accuse Hick of being selfish on this or any other occasion. I think time has been the healer between Hick and Atherton, and I'm sure Mike now knows that he was wrong. But he has to make the decisions and not all of them are going to be right. It was just that it went further than that. We wanted Graeme to play Test cricket for England for at least another four or five years, and things like that can break a player. As it is, Hick is now out of the Test picture with an average, in the mid thirties, that doesn't do justice to his ability. He had a very bad start to his England career but then did pretty well before he was dropped after a poor series against Pakistan. But I'm sure he'll come again. I don't think we've seen the last of Graeme Hick at Test level because he's a good enough player to force his way back. I hope he does, because he's a pillar of strength in most dressing-rooms he plays in. He doesn't want stardom. He just wants to get on with his cricket.

You do play the game for personal milestones. Of course, you want to be part of a winning and successful side, but you want to score as many Test hundreds or take as many Test five-fors as you can, and you must give players the opportunity to do that when you can. The effect it had on us that day was clear when we went out on the field. We bowled poorly and the Aussies had reached 139 without loss by the close, chasing a huge target. By the end of the fourth day, the bowlers were looking at each other thinking, 'Can they really pull this off? We're not going to be part of history again, are we?' If Australia had got 449 to win, they would certainly have created history; and the way Slater and Taylor were going that night, we didn't rule it out.

Day five
So much happened on the last day that I think it confirmed this Test as the best I have played in. There were so many fluctuations and so many points of interest. It was one of the most intense days that I have experienced, for sure. The public were certainly aware of the possibilities as 25,000 turned up.

Australia didn't score that freely in the first session, but they didn't lose a wicket, either, in getting to 206 by lunch. They were looking to get after me and I was nervous. I didn't feel ready for what was going to happen and I think they could detect that in me. At lunch, Phil Tufnell came up to me and said, 'They're going to get these runs. We're going to be part of history again.' I said, 'Shut up, Tuffers, try to be positive.' Then he'd disappear, say the same thing to someone else and appear at my shoulder again. Everyone was thinking it but no one else was saying it.

Then, just as the tension was mounting, it rained for quite a long time. Because, though, of the availability of the extra hour, we only lost seven overs and when we returned it was just like playing a one-day game, with Australia poised for a run chase. We had Tufnell to bowl over the wicket to pin them down if they started to threaten.

Umpire Darrell Hair had a bit of a shocker when we appealed for a run out to dismiss Taylor. He turned it down without calling for the third umpire, but the replays showed that Taylor was out. At least the rain had changed the wicket and I made the breakthrough by having Slater strangled, hooking to Tufnell who took a good catch on the boundary. It was only 208 for one but Australia's attitude changed after that and they shut up shop. It was almost as if they had pinned their hopes on Slater – if they were going to get the runs, he was going to be the one to do it for them. Now they seemed to realise that the rain had changed the wicket and buggered up their chances.

Taking a wicket gave me a boost and after that I bowled well at Boon and Taylor. I didn't get them out but I bowled with a lot more vigour, until I was taken off for a break. Funnily enough, I wasn't that fussed about bowling when I came back. I was tempted to almost go through the motions, because the game seemed destined for a draw. I thought it was a case, during a monster three-and-a-half-hour final session because of the earlier rain, of just bowling another four or five overs at them to keep them on their toes. But it turned out to be a lot more interesting than that.

I ended up bowling for an hour and a half, took four wickets for spit and bowled myself to a standstill. It was a great and enjoyable spell. I got both Waughs, Bevan and Healy as we staged a most unlikely victory bid. I had been getting some stick from the crowd earlier, but now, when things started going well, I was able to tell my tormentor, 'That's one more Test wicket than you'll ever get, pal.' Sydney has always been my second favourite venue, after Lord's, the crowd was big, my parents were there, I'd been written off and I had come back in style. It was one of those spells which don't come along too often, but with me, they seem to have occurred more often for England than Middlesex and I'm not complaining about that.

Taylor and Boon had also gone and we had them in real trouble at 292 for seven. But we just couldn't push on from there. Warne and Tim May put up a spirited resistance, I was absolutely shattered, my clothes saturated with sweat, and bad light was also coming into the reckoning. So we had to bring the spinners on and, unfortunately, Warne and May were able to play them out. By the close, I'd gone off because I got cramp diving to stop a ball – some of the lads panicked when they saw me in pain because they thought I'd done my hip again, but once they realised it was cramp they just laughed – and I got a nice ovation from the crowd. It was just a shame we couldn't finish the job, but it was a hell of a Test.

And one that ended in farcical circumstances, when the umpires took the teams off when the overs had been completed – except that the spinners were on and the final hour wasn't up, so Mike went and told them, as the covers were being pulled on, that the game wasn't over. So everybody trooped back, but still Warne and May couldn't be parted.

Gough was rightly named Man of the Match afterwards but I was in demand, too, for interviews and I had to bite my lip. While I was on the field, I'd been thinking, 'If anybody wants to speak to me, I'll have a go at the selectors,' but I thought better of it and just said the right things. I was delighted, but a bit down because we hadn't won and once again Australia had regained the Ashes. We had shown a bit of fight, which was much needed after the previous two Tests. When we went back to the hotel, I bought a couple of bottles of white wine and took them down to reception to drink with Atherton, Fairbrother, Gooch and others. Illingworth came down for a while with his wife, and I wrote: 'It was strange. He didn't say much to me, almost as if he wanted to avoid conversation. I tried to forget what had gone on before, but really I wanted to say, "Up yours, you northern git!" '

The interim

I'd gone ahead of a lot of the original bowlers in the party now. You have to be judged on merit once you join a tour, and I was back on the big scene. I woke up the day after Sydney knackered. It felt as though my body had been given a good kicking, but I only had one day to recover as we were off to Brisbane for the latest round of one-dayers, firstly against Zimbabwe. Due to my exertions in the Test, I was given this game off and spent a few hours on a day off with other players drinking Petaluma Riesling and sorting the world out. It's amazing how the best 'sessions' are never planned and just happen. This was one of them. Even though a few of us drank too much, we won comfortably in real heat. Graham Thorpe spent a night in hospital suffering from dehydration; it was that bad. We then played in front of 74,000 at Melbourne, the biggest crowd I've ever played in front of, but sadly we lost Gough to his foot injury. In this game we again won to give ourselves a chance of getting to the World Series finals and I took a career-best four for 22. Then we needed to get 237 against Australia A to reach the finals and it came down to me needing to score three off the final ball. Sometimes, as a tailender, you have to go in and get some runs and then if you don't, you feel it worse than anybody. I was nervous before I went out but concentrated on the task in hand when I was there until, unfortunately, I could only score one off Paul Reiffel and we were out of the competition.

It left Australia facing Australia A in the final, which was a bit of an anti-climax, particularly when some players started moving between the teams. By this time, Hick, Stewart and Fairbrother had all been added to the serious casualty list, Chris Lewis had joined us to replace Gough, even though he hadn't bowled for three months, and Ramprakash was on his way from the A tour in India. The dressing-room was like a hospital.

We had a few days off in Sydney while Australia were winning the one-day finals and we moved on to Bendigo, via Melbourne, where our injury crisis reached a peak when Dave Roberts, the physio, broke a finger. Even the physio was hurt now and he couldn't treat himself, let alone us.

By the time we got to Adelaide for the fourth Test, we

were struggling to put a side out. Lewis was virtually playing as a batsman and after the high of Sydney, lots of little things were happening that chipped away at us and no one gave us a chance of winning. Then, famously, Keith Fletcher said of our chances, 'You never know, lads. Stranger things have happened.' And they did.

Fourth Test, Adelaide Oval; 26–30 January 1995

Day one

We sang the national anthems before play, which was motivating. It's not something that is often done in cricket but I for one have always wanted to. One of the disappoint-ments of my Test debut was that there was no 'up and at 'em' speech or anything like that at all. We just went out there and I thought, 'Is that it? There's got to be more to it than that.' Playing the anthems pumps the players up and is something I'm sure a lot of people would welcome. I understand Graham Gooch wrote to the TCCB when he was captain requesting that it be considered, but he didn't even get a reply. It's not a question of being a royalist or nationalist, simply a recognition that you are representing your country. You want to hear the anthem before you go out.

There was a full house, which added to the sense of occasion. After singing the anthem, we went back in while the two batsmen stayed out to start the game. The pitch looked flat from the start and McDermott, who had bowled tremendously in the series, for once did not get among us. We had warmed up on what are probably the best practice facilities in the world. So many practice sessions before Tests degenerate into a half-hearted exercise, but not at Adelaide. They have grass, wide nets and full run-ups that create top-quality practice. Nets are so important to prepa-ration and you hardly ever get good ones in England. It is one of the things that we desperately need to correct.

We made a good start in the favourable conditions, with Gooch, Atherton and Gatting all prospering before a wind and then hailstorm hit us in mid-afternoon which made it seem that the world was coming to an end. We went back for a short while at the end of the day, with me padded up as nightwatchman, but we really shouldn't have done because the conditions were so bad. Still, at 196 for two by the close, we could be well happy.

Day two

We should have been looking for 450 today, but ended up with 353. The biggest plus for us was what turned out to be Mike Gatting's last century in Test cricket. He was dropped a couple of times and really had to grind the runs out, but I was delighted for Gatt, who has been such an important and ever-present figure to me and captain at Middlesex for most of my county career. He had struggled on this tour and I hadn't seen that happen too often. His response was to work hard at it until he got his reward at Adelaide, and he deserved that for not just giving in and accepting that his Test days were over.

Also, the Middlesex scorer Harry Sharp, a very popular figure and someone who was particularly close to Gatting, had died shortly before the match and Mike dedicated the century to him, which was a nice gesture. Mike Gatting is a straightforward bloke: what you see is what you get. He can be like a bull in a china shop at times, but over the years he's become a lot more guarded about what he says, because of the bad experiences he has had when being outspoken.

He has been outstanding throughout his career for Middlesex and is also the best captain I have played under. I say that because our dressing-room under Gatting has been the best working environment I've experienced. Some captains like to dominate and no one is allowed to raise their voices against them, but Gatting has always encouraged people to say what they want and get it off their chest. His philosophy has been to get any problem out into the open and then forget about it, which has worked very well for us.

We've had some massive rows over the years at Middlesex, but you turn up the next morning and it's like nothing happened. You just get on with life again. I wouldn't say Gatting is a particularly inspirational captain – I don't think I've ever played under one of them – but he leads by example and wants the team to follow. He's also tactically very sound. The amount of times he changes the bowling and then the new man gets a wicket in his first over is incredible. It can't always be luck, and over the years he has tended to get decisions right more often than most.

Gatt and I have had our moments – when you live with a group of blokes for such a long time, you are bound to cheese each other off from time to time – but he's good fun and I've enjoyed playing with him. He's never let a poor run of form affect his captaincy and has always turned up full of beans and enthusiasm for a day's play. He will never sulk or get moody about his own game, even when he struggles himself, and for a captain that's an important asset. Sure, he'll come in when he's out and throw his bat down, swear and curse and blame the wicket for his dismissal, but you know he'll be fine in an hour's time.

He has not been as good a player as Gooch or Gower. Mike's Test record is reasonable but it could have been a bit better. He does, after all, destroy county attacks and you would expect him to have averaged 40 in Tests, not in the mid 30s. Middlesex, however, could never complain that they haven't got their worth out of Mike Gatting. Year after year, he's got around 1,500 runs at 50, and while he hasn't reached those standards in his last couple of years, he was still contributing.

Some people said that he should have retired sooner, but it was not for me, nor anyone else at Middlesex, to tell him when to stop. It was for Mike to make that decision. If he was still enjoying himself and still thought that he could do a job, then he could carry on as far as I was concerned. In 1998 he retired having scored his thousand runs at 43, which a lot of people would be happy with, but for him it was considered a disappointment, which says a lot about his standards.

I didn't want to see Mike Gatting becoming a sorry figure, pretending to be what he was when he's not any more. It comes to us all and I hope I know when it's time for me to go. You have to get the timing right – Gooch, for example, may have gone a little early. A few people high up at Middlesex felt that Mike should have handed the captaincy over to Mark Ramprakash at the end of the 1996 season rather than in the middle of 1997, but I disagree. I think the timing of that one was perfect.

We've got a young side now and the players find it easier to relate to a younger person in charge. Gatting saw that and knew it was the time to hand over to Mark. Still, though, he couldn't help getting involved. When Ramprakash turned his back, for instance, Gatting would move a fielder a few yards here and a few yards there. He couldn't let go completely. He still wanted to be in control and have a certain amount of influence; that can make life a little hard for Mark, but he handled it very well.

Mike continued parking in the captain's space in the Lord's car park and sitting in the captain's chair at lunch. That's what he was like. He always wants to be in the thick of things and that includes being involved in the England set-up, currently as a selector and A team coach. What he may have to watch is his management of players. In the past, the Middlesex dressing-room has always been full of strong characters and they've been able to shrug it off when Mike has ranted and raved, but young players seem a lot more sensitive to criticism now. He may have to learn to handle people a bit differently, but there were signs, when he was encouraging players from slip in the 1997 season, that he is getting there.

He might have denied it, but he had a strong desire to reach 100 first-class hundreds, and eventually fell five short of the magic number. I thought, before the 1998 season, that if he didn't make a good start to the season, he might well retire halfway through it, but if he had a good year, he might even have played on for another one in pursuit of that target. Had that happened, and however much we may have thought, 'Gatt, it's time to go,' he had played for so long and done so much for the county that who were we to say he couldn't have another six months in the team?

Whenever Mike Gatting's name is mentioned, food is normally on the menu, too, and there's no doubt that he loves his grub. Eating with him is an experience. He's an expert on food, just as he is an 'expert' on everything. One day he was telling Jamie Hewitt how to bowl, then, when we got back to the dressing-room, he was watching tennis on TV and telling everyone where Tim Henman was going wrong with his serve. He knows everything about wine, saying this is crap and this is good, but normally he'll just pick out an expensive bottle and say, 'This'll be nice.'

He's certainly been through things. He's an instantly recognisable figure wherever he goes and has gone through stages of people loving and hating him, especially after the rebel tour of South Africa. He didn't really want to go on that 1989 trip but he went because he was so disillusioned about the way he had been treated by England. He wanted to say 'up yours' to the TCCB. Even though the money would also have been attractive to him, I know he had to think long and hard before deciding to go, because he loved playing for his country. Of course, he came back after that. He's not a tactful or eloquent person and he found himself in the middle of all these heavily political and dangerous situations, but it was typical of him to confront everything head-on. He never shirks an issue.

Soon after Adelaide, he announced, like Gooch, that he would end his Test career at Perth in the final match of the series. I think Gatting would have liked to carry on, but he realised, after a poor tour and at the age he was, that the writing was on the wall. It really was the end of an era with those two going. They were the last two survivors from the memorable England sides full of exciting players in the early eighties, but again, the timing was right. Whether his original selection for the tour was correct is another matter.

I was worried about Michael Slater when Australia replied. He always looks to get after me and it unsettles me. He's such a fine player that it's amazing he's dropped out of the Australian team now, with a Test average still in the fifties. He must have upset some influential people along the way. The manner in which he attacks the bowling, of course, has led to his shot selection being questioned, but to be honest, he didn't look the same player in 1997 when he was scratching around and not playing with the same freedom.

If you attack all the time, though, it can cause problems.

When things are going well and you're hitting the ball over mid-on and mid-off, everything is great. But when it doesn't come off, people will say, 'Sorry, you can't play that way,' and you suffer by going into your shell. At the start of their innings in this match, both Slater and Mark Taylor got after us and put us under pressure by reaching 81 without loss before the close. We knew that if those two got 150 past us, we'd be under a lot of pressure.

Day three
I really enjoyed this day, even though it was a bad one for us with Australia taking their score to 394 for five. I bowled well and reverse-swung the old ball despite the wicket being flat. I got Taylor out and things weren't going too badly until Greg Blewett and Ian Healy got going. We had two good sessions but the last one was terrible. I noted in my diary that Phil Tufnell had one of his days when he didn't really seem interested, which didn't help us either.

The cricket up to now had been competent without being truly intriguing, and the game seemed to have a draw written all over it.

Day four
Four years earlier, Mark Waugh had scored a hundred against us on his debut in Adelaide. This time, another Aussie did the same in Blewett. It's frightening when you see how regularly Aussies come in and grasp the game so quickly. When you compare it with how English players like Ramprakash, with all the talent in the world, struggle to make an immediate impact on the Test scene, it just speaks volumes for the Australian set-up and how well the

cricket below the top level prepares them for it. When they do play Test cricket, they seem to have a bit more about them. They don't walk in like a nervous teenager. They walk in expecting to do well.

Blewett played superbly, taking his overnight score of 91 to an unbeaten 102 as the Aussies were bowled out for 419. He was clearly a good puller and just looked so composed, like 'What's all the fuss about?' I made him work hard in the nineties, then he slogged me over gully to get to his hundred. But he looked good against quick bowling and only ever looked slightly less than comfortable when faced with spin. Healy had given him good support and the Aussies had a useful lead. I ended up with three for 95, which I was pleased with.

Things were tense when we batted again. I suppose it was what Test cricket was all about. Graham Thorpe played really well, or at least I'm told he did. As usual I didn't see a ball, being too nervous to do anything other than stay in the umpire's room in a nice comfortable armchair reading my book. I try to pretend there's not a game going on, try to relax and get away from it all. I also had a great thrill during this period of 'rest' when I met the legendary Don Bradman. I just bumped into him on the stairs in the middle of a stand. He came up and said: 'Hello, Angus, pleased to meet you.' For me this was a fantastic experience. We could only have chatted for around 30 seconds but it was like meeting royalty. Unfortunately, I have never met the Queen, even though I have played in four Lord's Tests and been to Buckingham Palace twice to be presented with the Lord's Taverners Trophy for winning the championship with Middlesex; on each occasion, she hasn't been there. I was to go on, the following year, to meet Nelson Mandela, but never the Queen. Maybe there's still time.

We finished up with our noses in front at 220 for six, with John Crawley and Phil DeFreitas in residence, but we felt more runs were needed if we were to be in a strong position.

Day five
After four fairly uneventful days, the game just exploded right at the start of the final day when Phil DeFreitas went berserk. At the start I had Australia as the favourites, but Phil played some thrilling shots, mainly off McDermott whom he took for 22 in one over. He and I put on 47 together after Crawley was out for 71, and I only got five of them. In half an hour, DeFreitas just took the game from them and handed it to us. We had started by thinking that if we could hang around and scratch a few more runs then it would mean they couldn't win, but suddenly that all dramatically changed as DeFreitas went bang, bang, bang.

An Englishman had, for once, seized the initiative and it was great fun to be at the other end while it was all going on. Australia were putting two out for the hook but he was just putting it over their heads. He was lifting them everywhere. DeFreitas has always had a good eye and when it comes off, he's a very dangerous hitter. Meanwhile, I tried to hook Mark Waugh and got out, and I wrote: 'This is getting to be a bad habit. People are starting to pepper me and I keep on saying I'll have a hook and keep on getting out. I must cut it out or everyone will be shoving it up me.'

When Phil hit Warne for an enormous six, we were heading towards a lead of 250 and the home side were cursing us. We ended up being bowled out for 328, leaving them 263 to win and us in an excellent position.

Then we got stuck into them. Australia never really looked as though they were going for the chase, when maybe the game was there for the taking if they really wanted to go for it. Devon bowled quick and they cracked under pressure. We had an amazing session just after lunch when we took four wickets in as many overs, Devon getting three of them and really shaking Steve Waugh up before bowling him with a rapid ball. I strangled Boon down the leg side with a long hop that he got a glove on, and I thought, 'I'll take that.'

We had a bit of luck, too, when Mark Waugh was caught out cutting a ball that rebounded off Gatting's toe and into his hands, and we generally worked our way through their batting order. Only Healy and Damien Fleming then hung around making nuisances of themselves, but we kept on fighting and eventually, the leg-spinning debutant Peter McIntyre was the last out to a slightly questionable LBW and we had bowled them out for 156. Incredible. From a position on the first day when we went on to the field with a threadbare side and the words 'You never know, stranger things have happened' in our ears, we had turned the whole thing round and won the game. OK, it may have been a case of the Australians taking their foot off the pedal with the Ashes already won, but it was still a notable achievement by us and I wouldn't belittle it in any way.

Chris Lewis had done extremely well to come from holiday and take four wickets in that second innings. Part of his match fee was taken from him for a gesture he made in sending McDermott on his way after the pair had had a bit of a run-in, but I'm not against a bowler showing a bit of aggression in that way. Poor Chris can't win. If he doesn't show any emotion, people say he's too laid-back and doesn't care enough; but then when he shows a bit of aggression and gets a bit animated, he gets himself in trouble for 'over-reacting'. Match referees' decisions are a bit of a lottery at the moment. I think on the whole it's good that we have them – even if it is a bit of a jobs-for-the-boys affair – but we need consistency in their decisions for the system to work properly.

We had quite an evening of celebration after the match. It started at the ground, carried on at our hotel and then continued at a bar, with the Barmy Army. I'm told I was up on a table singing at one point with the fans, but I can't remember that. What I do remember is that it was my first Test win in Australia. Jack Russell did another 'Moment of Victory' painting and gave a few copies of it to each of the players, in return for us signing them all. Then we heard that a group of England supporters had run into travel problems and, to make sure they got to Perth in time for the next Test, had left Adelaide early on the final day. They had sat through four days of average Test cricket and then missed all the fun – and all to see us get thrashed at Perth. I didn't know whether to laugh or cry for them.

The aftermath

We had a bad time in the final Test at Perth. Ramprakash came in for another casualty and played well, but Crawley and DeFreitas bagged pairs and Gooch and Gatting, who were each given three cheers by the Australian side on their arrivals at the wicket, both bowed out on low notes. Blewett scored an even better hundred than in Adelaide and Steve Waugh was left stranded on 99 when his brother, acting as a runner, ran out his final partner. That was funny.

At the end of it, I was left on 99 Test wickets, which annoyed me hugely, and the series had ended as it started: with us being thrashed. I wrote: 'I suppose it is apt that the tour finished as it had been for much of the time – a bit of a shambles.' We flew home and, on arrival, all waited for Atherton to pick up his luggage and lead us through the arrivals gate to face the music. MJK Smith finished on a high. He was supposed to have ordered cars for us all, but they didn't turn up so I had to queue outside Terminal Four for a cab home, which cost me £35. Well done, manager!

Having not been selected in the first place – such a blow to me – and then been called up, doing so well while I was there was very satisfying. But overall, this was the most disappointing tour I'd been on. It wasn't helped by the unbelievable injury list, but the tour had never got going. It just wasn't the happiest of trips. There was too much going on. Clearly Illingworth and Fletcher weren't getting on and that spread through the team. I was delighted to have achieved something and proved a few people wrong, but it was so annoying that we hadn't got it right from the word go again. Too often we start slowly and struggle to make something of the tour in the last few weeks. It was soul-destroying. I remember sitting up in the middle of the night listening to the Gatting tour of Australia in 1986–87, when we virtually destroyed them. Yet subsequently, the Aussies have thrashed us and they are clearly the best side in the world, as they proved again in retaining the Ashes in 1997.

There's not an area of their side that you would call weak. The Ashes are the biggest series you can play in and at the moment we're just not up there with them. We always seem to go to Australia with quite a bit of optimism, but they just knock us down. They're very aggressive, very competitive and are unrelenting in their cricket, in your face all the time. They can't do enough for you off the field, but on it in whatever match it is, they are going to try to stuff you. I think the way to try to bridge the gap is to emulate much of what they do. But so many in our game believe our old system will work again one day.

People seem to think that in the 'good old days' we used to beat them regularly, but as Micky Stewart points out, we have never had that much success against them. I find it unbelievable when I hear that Alec Bedser was supposed to have said, on hearing of Lord MacLaurin's appointment as chairman of the ECB, that you wouldn't find him (Bedser) running Tesco's, so why should MacLaurin run cricket? Could you imagine Lord MacLaurin going to his share-holders and saying, 'Yes, we haven't done anything this year but don't worry, it's cyclical and the methods we use will come back into fashion again one day.' They would say out you go, mate. We can't just sit back, do bugger-all and think things will change in our favour, because they won't. We simply have to change the structure of our cricket, and we missed a golden opportunity to do that in 1997 by rejecting the chance to have two divisions of the county championship. There are not many people who have played for England in recent times who would disagree with that. But the counties voted for no change, and as a result, the game is going nowhere.

Cricket is just so much more ruthless in Australia. They don't leave anything to chance. If their game is not working for the betterment of the national side, then they will just change things. They won't ask the states if they'd like change. It's the same in their other sports, and they are generally better than us at rugby and other things. Their general attitude and the way they prepare over there is something we should look at immediately. A lot of our county professionals go over there during our winters and end up playing second- or third-grade cricket because they can't make it in first-grade, which is bloody serious. It means that their club players are better than a lot of our pros.

Grade cricket is a bloody hard school, and to get through it you have to get a lot of things right. Meanwhile, our counties are very keen to sign their fringe players, people like Stuart Law, Darren Lehmann and Michael Bevan, and they proceed to come over here and dominate, showing how good they are and how frightening it is that they're not good enough for the Australian Test side. Something has to change in our game. The Aussies changed when we were beating them and although it took time, they got it right. If Lord MacLaurin gets frustrated and walks away from our game, we'll be in big trouble, because he's a top man who could do immense good if given the chance. If he disappeared, I'm sure a lot of the money in the game would disappear with him. Australia are the leaders of our sport, while in England there's so much self-interest and history that stops us moving forward. Counties accept their big hand-outs from the profits of Test cricket, but won't do anything in return. It's not good enough.

England to Australia 1994–95

First Test
Woolloongabba, Brisbane, 25, 26, 27, 28, 29 November
Australia 426 (M.J.Slater 176, M.E.Waugh 140, M.A.Taylor 59) and 248 for 8 dec (M.A.Taylor 58)
England 167 (M.A.Atherton 54, C.J.McDermott 6 for 53) and 323 (G.A.Hick 80, G.P.Thorpe 67, G.A.Gooch 56, S.K.Warne 8 for 71)
Result: Australia won by 184 runs.

Second Test
Melbourne Cricket Ground, 24, 26, 27, 28, 29 December
Australia 279 (S.R.Waugh 94 not out, M.E.Waugh 71) and 320 for 7 dec (D.C.Boon 131)
England 212 (G.P.Thorpe 51, S.K.Warne 6 for 64) and 92 (C.J.McDermott 5 for 42)
Result: Australia won by 295 runs.

Third Test
Sydney Cricket Ground, 1, 2, 3, 4, 5 January
England 309 (M.A.Atherton 88, J.P.Crawley 72, D.Gough 51, C.J.McDermott 5 for 101) and 255 for 2 dec (G.A.Hick 98 not out, M.A.Atherton 67)
Australia 116 (D.Gough 6 for 49) and 344 for 7 (M.A.Taylor 113, M.J.Slater 103, A.R.C.Fraser 5 for 73)
Result: Match drawn.

Fourth Test
Adelaide Oval, 26, 27, 28, 29, 30 January
England 353 (M.W.Gatting 117, M.A.Atherton 80) and 328 (P.A.J.DeFreitas 88, G.P.Thorpe 83, J.P.Crawley 71, M.E.Waugh 5 for 40)
Australia 419 (G.S.Blewett 102 not out, M.A.Taylor 90, I.A.Healy 74, M.J.Slater 67) and 156 (I.A.Healy 51 not out)
Result: England won by 106 runs.

Fifth Test
W.A.C.A. Ground, Perth, 3, 4, 5, 6, 7 February
Australia 402 (M.J.Slater 124, S.R.Waugh 99 not out, M.E.Waugh 88) and 345 for 8 dec (G.S.Blewett 115, S.R.Waugh 80, M.A.Taylor 52)
England 295 (G.P.Thorpe 123, M.R.Ramprakash 72) and 123 (C.J.McDermott 6 for 38)
Result: Australia won by 329 runs.

Angus Fraser's tour (3rd, 4th and 5th Tests):
Batting: 5 innings, 0 not out, high score 27, runs 53, average 10.60.
Bowling: 129.5 overs, 25 maidens, 389 runs, 14 wickets, average 27.78, best 5–73.

england in south africa 1995–96

The background

Returning from Perth on 99 Test wickets was a huge disappointment. The 100-wicket landmark was one that I desperately wanted to reach. But it had been a long year or so, and I was looking forward to having some time off. I didn't do a great deal in the build-up to the season. There was a change in selectors, with David Graveney being elected, and the powers-that-be were gradually working towards having younger men on board, something that virtually all the players thought necessary.

Then Keith Fletcher was sacked by the Board as team manager, which was sad. As I said, it was obvious that he and Illingworth didn't get on, and clearly Illingworth thought Fletcher at fault for a lot of the things that had gone wrong. A scapegoat was, as ever, needed and the Board decided that Fletcher was the man to carry the can. I enjoyed working with Keith. I'm pretty easy-going about what I expect from a manager and feel I should be able to get myself motivated playing for England, but maybe some of the more demanding players needed a stronger character. Fletcher is a quiet bloke who did not generally enjoy getting up in front of a group of players making big speeches. He was far happier working one-to-one with someone and got very intense about our cricket, so much so that he was almost a nervous wreck by the end of each tour.

He found out about his sacking when he rang Lord's from a skiing holiday, which, as so often, was a very clumsy way of handling the matter. After the news was made public, a few papers sent their reporters off to hunt Keith down somewhere in the Alps to try to get his story, but I don't think they had much success in their mission of finding a gnome-like character on the slopes. At least Fletcher was in the middle of a long-term contract, which he had sought to give himself some security after leaving what Essex had told him would be a job for life with them, so he didn't leave England empty-handed. But he had always seemed to back me and I enjoyed working with him, so I was saddened by it all. Ray Illingworth, meanwhile, was now England's first 'supremo'.

I had a good time in the build-up to the 1995 season. I watched Liverpool, saw a few rugby internationals and went to Paris for a Graham Gooch benefit trip. Then Middlesex went off to Portugal again for our pre-season trip, which provided another opportunity for everybody to get to know each other and talk about the season over a glass of red.

The West Indies were our visitors that summer and I was in the squad for the one-day internationals against them at the end of May. I bowled straight at Trent Bridge, without looking like getting wickets, and then Peter Martin replaced me for the second international at The Oval. By this time we had gained our first glimpse of Illingworth in a tracksuit, because now he had a hands-on role. But I wrote that I didn't think he really knew what to do while we were warming up – he even joined in the stretching exercises at one point. Around this time, I'd go through spells when I didn't think Illy was such a bad bloke after all, and then he'd say something in the press again that I'd shake my head at.

We won the one-dayers 2–1, which was a good start to the summer and it had been another enjoyable week spent at three different venues preparing for the bigger challenges of the Test series ahead.

Then, just after I thought I'd proved myself in Australia, I was left out of the first Test. I wrote: 'They're playing Devon for his extra pace. When Athers walked over to me in the nets, I thought he was going to walk straight past, but he didn't. I still can't believe they think there are better bowlers than me.' As Atherton left the dressing-room that day at Headingley, he was talking with someone about the world rankings and he asked me where I stood in them. My reply reflected the mood I was in. 'A lot higher than anyone else in this team,' I said. 'On your head be this.' He later told me he couldn't get my words out of his head all day.

We bowled poorly in that match and got stuffed, and I returned for the second Test at Lord's. The match was played on a wicket that received a lot of stick because it was cracked, but it actually produced an excellent Test. The best games are often the ones when the ball is slightly on top of the bat, though you would never guess that from the batsman-friendly legislation that has been brought into the game in recent years.

Anyway, Dominic Cork made his debut and I, at last, got my 100th Test wicket: Brian Lara, LBW, so it was a pretty good one. Steve Waugh was my first Test wicket and Brian Lara my 100th, and it meant an awful lot. After I missed the first Test, the thought did occur to me that I might end my career on 99 wickets, which would have been painful. I look at *Wisden* a lot and I desperately wanted to see my name there among the leading bowlers, and you have to get 100 Test wickets for that. Before the 1997–98 tour to West Indies, I needed four wickets to overtake Ray Illingworth, which was something else I was pleased to do!

When I got Lara out, the landmark was announced over the Tannoy and I walked down to fine leg, not exactly expecting an ovation but hoping I might be greeted with at least a ripple. Instead, I got an England supporter shouting, 'Oi, Fraser, you tosser. What did you do that for? I haven't spent £35 to watch you bowling all day.' I thought, 'Thanks a lot.' There I was busting a gut trying to win a Test for England and all this bloke wanted was to see Lara smash me around all day.

We went on to earn a very good win. Cork took seven wickets in the second innings and exploded onto the England scene. My views on Dominic Cork have changed since then – and I have to say we have had our moments, particularly later in South Africa – but at that time I thought he wasn't such a bad lad and that perhaps he'd been a bit misunderstood. He was clearly very motivated and his confidence would have built up quickly after the summer he continued to have after Lord's.

The series proved to be a highly entertaining one, with four magnificent Tests swinging it this way and that. At Edgbaston we were steamrollered, controversially, early on the third day, and I remember sitting in the dressing-room after the West Indies had won convincingly, looking out at an angry crowd and almost being apprehensive about going outside, worrying about the response we were going to get. When I eventually walked round the ground some harsh things were said to me, and I could understand the public's reaction because there was no excuse for the way we played. OK, it was a bad wicket and it played into their hands to a certain extent, but you have to remember that Curtly Ambrose was injured early on, so the West Indies weren't at full strength. Even so, I was concerned enough about the conditions, when I went in to bat, to ask Richard Illingworth what it was like out there. 'I've just faced the fastest ball I've seen for a long, long time,' he said. That was just what I wanted to hear!

To compound the disappointment of that defeat, Middlesex asked me to head straight to Bristol to play in the Sunday league the day afterwards. I rang them up to see how they all were, hardly expecting them to call on my services – but they did, which didn't go down too well at home. This, remember, was the Test after Lord's, when I had immediately had to leave after the match to travel six hours to Cornwall for the following day's NatWest Trophy tie. It seems that England players have no time to enjoy the good times or reflect on the bad ones before we're off on the county circuit again.

Then followed Old Trafford, when, with Cork producing a hat-trick, we squared the series at 2–2, which seemed to set the series up for a thrilling finale at Trent Bridge and The Oval. But what happened? They produced totally flat batting pitches so that it just fizzled out and the series ended in stalemate. I thought, 'What's the point of that? Everyone's had a great summer and now it's been allowed to finish in anti-climax.' It was a shame.

With Middlesex finishing second in the championship, I had had a hectic summer and it was catching up on me. I was left out of the first Test but was selected for England's first tour of South Africa since their readmission to Test cricket. It was an appetising prospect.

The build-up

I had never been to South Africa before. I had the opportunity, when I was younger, to play a season for Orange Free State as their overseas player and I thought long and hard about going. The offer came in 1988 after I'd got 80 wickets and it seemed to be a sensible next step in my cricketing education, but at that time there were a lot of noises about sanctions for anyone who went there and I didn't want to do anything that might be held against me in future years.

I wasn't sure what to do, so I went to see AC Smith of the TCCB at Lord's to ask his advice. We had a meeting, but I came away none the wiser about the situation. I didn't think I was completely safe, so I turned it down – but I wish I'd done it in many ways, because I would have liked to have played a season's first-class cricket abroad to see what it was like. As it was, I ended up playing grade cricket in Sydney, so that was still beneficial and very enjoyable.

People who had been to South Africa built it up as a great tour and I was looking forward to seeing the country, but I didn't really know what to expect. As soon as I arrived, though, the contrasts between the haves and the have-nots, usually decided by colour, were strikingly evident. Maybe I wasn't quite ready for what I saw.

When we got there, it was as if we had travelled for ten hours just to reach Manchester. It was raining heavily in Johannesburg and was pretty cold, but my initial impression was that South Africa looked like a cross between

Australia and India. It was a big country with lots of space, but poverty was never very far away. We were greeted by some dancers, who were great, and I wrote that I was sure Illy would make the headlines the next day because, in the press conference, he had called our welcoming party 'a bunch of Zulus jumping around'.

It was also evident straight away that as far as the South Africans were concerned, we were not just there for the cricket. We were there to help them get things right politically. I had mixed feelings about all this. I thought we should have been focusing on the cricket, not making political statements, but it was clear that Ali Bacher of the South African Board was a nice but also very shrewd and cunning man. I wrote: 'I get the feeling that things are still very fragile here.' Steve Tshwete, the minister for sport, spoke to us and it was hard to fully appreciate what he, as a former inmate of Robben Island, and others had been through for the sake of their country and their people. He was clearly a very brave man.

We were warned to be very careful in Johannesburg and introduced to our security guard, Rory, who was to be with us at all times. He told us never to go out alone in Jo'burg, never to stop at a red light if we were driving at night, and various other safety measures. We had been aware, in a few other places I had been to with England, like Kingston, Jamaica, of the need to be careful, but never in the same way that we were warned about Jo'burg. It was quite worrying.

Driving from the airport to the hotel was the first time I had seen a township, which made me think what a lucrative job being a barbed-wire salesman in South Africa must be. That is not being flippant, it is simply a way of emphasising the conditions so many people were forced to live under out there. They were just awful, with whole families living in a single room, and the contrast between the places I saw en route and then the conditions at Sandton, where we were staying, was incredible. There we found huge houses and obvious wealth, but even then you could see what an intimidating place we were in because there were huge walls topped with barbed wire around each of the affluent properties. Basically, the white people still have the money in post-apartheid South Africa and the black people want a slice of it. The crime rate is bloody high.

We stayed at the Sandton Sun, which was a great hotel, and I had my first experience of training at altitude. I had a burning sensation in my throat when I finished but it wasn't really as bad as I expected. Then the first of those promotional and political duties to which I was referring took place, when we went to the township of Alexandria to open a new pavilion. More than 300,000 people live in a square mile there, and when we arrived we were told that if we had been any earlier we would have heard gunfire, because there was a running gun battle going on. The people's lives seemed so deprived to me, yet they were so proud of this new pavilion and so happy that we were there with them. It was humbling.

I was robbed early on in our stay. There were safes in the hotel rooms but one day I forgot to put my wallet in mine and instead left it in my jeans pocket. When I returned, all my money, around £100 in rand, had been taken but my wallet was left there, and when I mentioned it to John Barclay, the tour manager, it became clear that a few other players had been robbed, too. Understandably, the manager didn't want to make a fuss, so he asked me not to mention it to anyone, but it was horrible to think of someone, presumably a hotel employee, going through my pockets each day until they found something.

Further 'good news' came when Denise rang me to tell me to send my driving licence home because I'd been caught speeding by a camera while rushing to The Oval towards the end of the season. That was another three penalty points I could have done without.

Things improved when we visited the home of Nicky Oppenheimer, one of South Africa's wealthiest men, for drinks and a barbecue. It was a beautiful house, with a library that contained books of South Africa's accounts over hundreds of years, in a wood-panelled cabinet behind glass doors on shelves. It seems his family controlled business in South Africa to an enormous extent. We played a game at Oppenheimer's ground, which is like a South African version of John Paul Getty's ground in Wormsley. Whereas Getty's lovely country ground is quintessentially English, Oppenheimer's was typically South African, a lot louder and more up front. His son went to university here and is a good club cricketer, so he was a member of the Oppenheimer XI that we faced and we had a gentle tour opener, a sort of South African Arundel or Lilac Hill. At this game I met Vintcent van der Bijl, an outstanding South African bowler who spent one summer as Middlesex's overseas player before my time. He was an enormous but gentle man and someone I think Middlesex hoped I would emulate.

I had been told that the wickets would suit me in South Africa because they would have pace and bounce, but even at this early stage I was beginning to wonder if that was strictly true. Illingworth was, by now, at the centre of most things and had already decided to travel to the grounds by car instead of on the coach with us because he couldn't stand the loud music that Wayne Morton, the physio, liked to play on our team stereo. Devon Malcolm had already received a ticking-off for his attitude towards the bowling coach Peter Lever – a taste of things to come – while we all took the chance to buy a couple of copies each of Nelson Mandela's autobiography, which Rory told us he could get signed later in the tour.

Then we prepared to play in Soweto, the South West Township, as the name is short for. I wrote: 'Today is strange. I am aware that we are going to a dangerous area. We needed an escort all the way there and it is quite a drive from where we are staying. I wonder what is in store.' Yet when we arrived, everybody was waving to us and seemed delighted to see us. Again, in some ways it was a diversion from the tour, because we weren't really gaining cricket-wise from being there, but it was an eye-opening experience. I was just worried that we were being used politically. I thought back to the Mike Gatting rebel tour of 1989 and how he wasn't trained to do and say the right things in acutely sensitive political situations. Now I was worried that something any of us said might have been misconstrued or taken out of context, because we were, after all, sportsmen, not diplomats.

But it was fine, and this turned out to be the day we met Nelson Mandela. We were told that he might well pop in sometime during the game and we were all looking forward to that, but we didn't expect it to be on the first day and, consequently, I didn't have my camera on me. I really wished I had brought it when he arrived, because there are few heroes in this world and he is definitely one of them.

My knees went weak when I met him, it was just the most amazing thing. I've never seen so many people so focused on one person. Nobody took their eyes off him. Nobody spoke to each other while he was at the ground. Who knows how Atherton and Stewart, who were batting at the time, managed to concentrate on the game and stop themselves getting out, because it was like a god had walked into the ground and was among us. Everyone, without exception, was aware that someone special was in our midst.

I didn't know what to say to Mandela when I was introduced to him. He told me, because of my size, that I was intimidating him and that he didn't know how their cricketers felt about playing against me. He then asked if I was enjoying the country. I just muttered that I was pleased to meet him. He's actually taller than you think and also looked really well for his age, and considering all he has been through in his life. He just seemed such a gentle, kind, lovable man. Then he, famously, said to Devon, 'I know you, you're the destroyer,' a reference to Devon's nine wickets at The Oval in 1994. It must have been unbelievable for Devon.

I felt privileged to be there. Lunch lasted a lot longer than usual and then the president did a lap of the ground with Devon while a group of us followed them in a huddle, walking five yards behind. Mandela was like a magnet and we just wanted to watch him and hear what he had to say. And if we were thrilled, I can only imagine what it must have been like for the children of Soweto to have the great man among them. Soon after, he was back in his car and away. One of life's best experiences was over and the cricket seemed a total anti-climax after that.

I know how I felt about it all, but it is impossible for me

to know what it must have been like for a black person to spend time with Nelson Mandela. It must have been so emotional for Devon and the whole thing did affect him, you could tell that. Illingworth, as we know, thought that Devon became preoccupied and wasn't concentrating on his cricket. Whether their board were using him or not, I don't know, but we had done a lot of PR stuff for them and there was a feeling that Devon's mind was more on that than the cricket. But what followed was quite terrible handling of a player who should have been our biggest psychological weapon in the build-up to the Test series.

First, Devon was sent to bowl in the nets for an extra session because he hadn't bowled that well in the match. It seemed harsh to me and it became a bit of a power thing, with the management flexing their muscles and dictating to Devon. He also had a problem with his knee, which didn't help, but it was his relationship with the management that was causing the most concern. I wrote in my diary: 'Dev is not getting on with Illy and something is going to happen soon.' The dispute then hit the papers big time, with Lever reported as saying that Devon was 'a cricketing nonentity' apart from his pace. The players couldn't believe some of the things that were being said. Devon had really shaken South Africa up at The Oval in 1994. All right, his performances since then had been up and down, but even so, we weren't using the advantage we had over South Africa. It must have been on their minds going into the series.

Illingworth wanted Lever to work with Devon because he was frustrated with his inconsistencies, which, really, was fair enough. But Devon's knee was hurting, there was the Mandela business, and Devon is how he is – an easy-going man, not aggressive or confrontational, who just wanted to get on with what had brought him his success up to then. At the end of the day, Devon Malcolm has more Test wickets than Ray Illingworth or Peter Lever, so he must be doing something right. The management took his laid-back approach to mean that he wasn't interested, and wondered what they could do to rectify the situation. But in getting heavy-handed, they undermined our biggest weapon in that series and it just wasn't a clever thing to do. Of course, they should never have criticised him publicly. That suggested to our hosts that there was turmoil in our side before we'd even started. It didn't do us any favours at all and must have brought a smile to their faces.

From Soweto we went to East London, where the process of getting to know our new tourists continued. It was the first time I had been away with a number of our players, like Mark Ilott, Mike Watkinson, Peter Martin, Richard Illingworth and Dominic Cork, so I was still finding out what they were like. Dominic, of course, was big and getting bigger, but the others were all good company who were quietly (or in Ilott's case loudly) getting on with their jobs and being good tourists.

Around this time, Graham Thorpe had to fly home to be with his wife, who had a personal problem, and for once the management handled the situation really well and were very understanding, telling him to take as long as he needed. At the same time, I was starting to feel a bit lonely for one of the few occasions I can remember on tour. Sometimes on a tour you get fed up of going out every night and would like to sit down in your armchair at home with your family. I'm sure every player must go through this at some stage of a tour, and this was my time.

From quiet East London we moved on to very hot

Kimberley. There was also a strong wind blowing and as soon as I got out of the plane one of the guys turned to me and said, 'I know which end you're bowling from, Gus!' It was roasting there. We went to a local school to practise and again the facilities were better than in England, such an important aspect of a cricketer's preparation. Devon was particularly impressive in the nets and everyone was talking about how fast he was bowling. But there was a reason. The net was about seven feet high at the back and Illingworth was standing behind it in a wicketkeeper's position, watching what was going on. Devon was bowling rapidly because he was trying to bowl bouncers that would go over the top of the net and hit our supremo. Illingworth was standing there, arms crossed, with no idea what was going on, thinking that Devon had finally started to listen to him and was bowling accordingly. And the poor batsmen were getting peppered.

Atherton and I had our usual competitive word in the nets and on this occasion, the press thought our aggression was for real. You tend to try that much harder against good mates and I have often had words with Athers in practice but it's all in jest, to get yourself going. We thought it was hilarious that the press were contemplating portraying it as an 'incident', so we planned to start wagging our fingers at each other hoping they would write it up the next day. But they didn't in the end.

I spoke to Denise on the phone from Kimberley for about 30 minutes and it cost me £30, an indication of how much you can spend on phone calls home during a tour. I can easily get through £1,000 just by routinely calling every few days, and I was pleased to hear that the players on the Zimbabwe and New Zealand tour the following year had been given an allowance for phone calls. Mind you, that was probably only because wives and families had been banned from the tour.

I lost 8lb during a day's play in Kimberley, even though I took on plenty of fluids, but gained my first first-class wicket on the tour – always something of a relief, because every bowler remembers that Phil DeFreitas once went through a whole tour without one. Also on this leg of the tour, Wayne Morton's wife gave birth to a little boy and Graham Thorpe rejoined us, quiet but seemingly OK after his visit home.

We were also introduced to Paul Adams, the left-arm wrist spinner with an amazing action, who bowled us out in this game. I faced him for quite a while, never quite knowing where the ball was going to go.

Then the build-up to the first Test began. Even though we were playing in Centurion, just outside Pretoria, we stayed in Johannesburg. We were put in to bat on a wicket that looked a little damp, but Atherton and Hick both did well and we had got ourselves into a reasonable position on the second day before an enormous storm hit the ground soon after we came off for lightning. Their players and umpire Cyril Mitchley were very concerned about the lightning and were very quick to come off – and off we stayed for the rest of the game, with us on 381 for nine.

The ground was never fit for play after that, condemning me to the first and so far only wicketless Test of my career. I couldn't be too hard on myself about that, because I didn't bowl a ball and when people said to me then that I'd got 119 wickets in 32 Tests, I was always tempted to say 31 because there was little I could do to add to my total in this match.

The weather was a great shame. There had been a big build-up to this first Test between these sides in South Africa since their readmission, and there had been no rain in the area for months. Then this happens. In some ways, we left the Test encouraged because they had got a renowned pace attack and we had coped pretty well with it. But from then on, the tour went downhill for me.

For a start, there was only one more game before the Johannesburg Test, a match that we knew would be pivotal in the series because the wicket was expected to have pace and bounce and provide a result. So with that in mind, it was vital that we used the game in Bloemfontein against Orange Free State to get things right. The management were planning to field four pace bowlers in the second Test and wanted to use this game almost as a trial between Devon, Peter Martin and Mark Ilott for the final place. So even though I was keen to play in Bloemfontein and get some overs under my belt, I had to miss out and spent the time frantically bowling in net sessions, not the sort of practice I needed.

The Orange Free State match ended up going nowhere and, remarkably, they called it off and had a one-day game at the end of it instead. So I did get six overs in a match situation, but they did me no good at all. There was a huge brawl among the crowd at the end of the one-dayer, with police dogs being needed, but they didn't seem to mind a punch-up in South Africa. The people, on the whole, were pretty aggressive in their character. I know it's a gross generalisation, but the people in Orange Free State did live up to their image of being rough and ready, and we even had the unpleasant experience of hearing some of them making racist comments about Devon in a bar there. There were still lots of signs of the old days in this part of the country.

We travelled on to Jo'burg, where Rory the security guard pulled off a great practical joke on Wayne Morton. Earlier, when Wayne had offered to treat Rory for a knee problem he had, the physio whitewashed Rory's leg and Rory said, 'I'll get you back for that.' And he did, in some style. As we came through the airport, Wayne was 'arrested' by the narcotics police, made to identify his bags, handcuffed and driven away. John Barclay, who was in on the joke, was very serious when he was called in by the police, and Wayne was starting to worry about things when he was then rough-ridden across town in the back of a police van. But when it stopped and Wayne was let out, we were all there to greet him. He admitted to being worried a couple of times, but took the whole thing well.

We had nets at Centurion Park because they were better than the ones at the Wanderers, and I was struggling a bit with a groin injury. It turned out to be Gilmour's Groin and I needed an operation at the end of the tour for it, but for now it wasn't serious enough to stop me playing. Sometimes you just have to play through these things as a bowler, or you would never get on the park. There was also, during practice, a row between Cork and Gough and I wrote, tongue in cheek: 'I don't think Johannesburg is big enough for the both of them.'

Second Test, The Wanderers, Johannesburg, 30 November–4 December 1995

Day one

The Test started with me worrying about my fitness and being short of practice anyway, consequently I didn't bowl very well. But Cork did a great job after we had put them in to bat and we got late wickets which saved our faces a bit. I spent most of the day bowling to Gary Kirsten, who played very well for his 110, and I was guilty of bowling too straight and getting worked through the leg side. My figures in my last two Tests at home had not been very good, and suddenly I was getting worried about having three bad Tests in a row and my place coming under threat.

But the pitch was pretty flat and I didn't think we had made the right decision in putting them in. They finished the day on 278 for seven and a few of the guys went off to a Bon Jovi concert. I gave it a miss and rang Denise to cheer myself up and seek consolation, and she just told me to do my best, that was all I could do.

Despite my lack of success, I actually thought that this was close to being the best wicket I had played Test cricket on. It played consistently, but there was a bit of bounce and if you bowled well, you had a chance. But I didn't bowl well. I was also hugely impressed with the Wanderers, which was an impressive stadium. After Lord's and Sydney, it ranks up there with the best I've seen.

Mike Atherton seemed a bit low and I couldn't work out why, because he had done pretty well in the first Test. As a friend, I wondered if I was giving him enough support, but I thought his mood might have been down to the fact that he realised he'd made a mistake in putting them in.

Day two

We played very poorly. They began the day by hitting out well to take their score to 332 and I got slapped for 23 off the four overs I bowled. It was typical of the way things were going for me. I ended up wicketless from 20 overs, while Cork took five wickets and Malcolm four. Then to compound my personal misery, I was out for a duck and got stacks of stick walking up the chicken run to the dressing-room. I felt like thumping them as I took the abuse, and I could see why Merv Hughes had got into a bit of trouble here when he had a go back at a supporter during an Australian visit. People on both sides of the thing were screaming and banging on advertising boards, and it wasn't very pleasant.

We were all out for 200, a long way behind, and only Robin Smith reached 50 for us. Alec Stewart and Jonty Rhodes had a few words during play, with Alec suggesting that Jonty was only in the team because of his fielding. It must have hit a nerve, because Jonty was still upset about it when we came off. By this time, I felt so low that I couldn't get any lower and started to think positively: if we could bowl them out for 150, then we'd have a chance. I was also being realistic, though, and wrote: 'I bet the rain doesn't come now.'

I couldn't help thinking that my Test place was on the line. I had a chat with Atherton about it and he told me that I was bowling OK but that the odd four-ball was creeping into my game. I, for my part, thought that I hadn't bowled enough and was lonely and low. I kept myself to myself but had a good chat with John Crawley, who told me to keep it in perspective and just give it my best shot. Your moods do change on tour. When you do well, you're confident and noisy and want to go out, but when it's going badly, you do go into your shell. It was something I had to sort out on my own.

Day three

They worked themselves into a marvellous position and God knows what they were doing coming off early for bad light in the position they were in. We felt we'd have been crucified if we'd done the same. It just emphasised what a defensive side they were. South Africa talked positively and in an upbeat fashion, but they were actually very defensive and their first priority was definitely not to lose. Throughout the tour, they didn't stamp their authority on us as much as they should have done, but even so, we were still in a mess when they came off more than 400 ahead at 296 for six, with Brian McMillan unbeaten on 76.

I bowled well this time and on a luckier day could have got a few more wickets than the two, Andrew Hudson and Jonty Rhodes, that I bagged. I enjoyed bowling at McMillan. He's the king of the sledgers but very amusing with it. Because I liked and admired the bloke, we tended to have the odd word but it was never anything serious; if it had been, he would probably have filled me in behind the stand afterwards!

McMillan kept on nudging and nurdling me down to third man, and I asked him if he had any shots in front of square. He'd say, in his best sarcastic voice, 'Oh, you're just too quick for me.' Sometimes, if you can have a little exchange, it keeps you on your toes and keeps you going when it's not going well for you. It's never nasty. You just try to get a little more out of yourself.

Each evening, we tended to watch the highlights of the

Australia v Pakistan series on television and I thought, 'Haven't we all had enough of cricket by this time of day?' I suppose it shows, though, that you have to love the game in the first place to play it. The wicket had not deteriorated as much as we thought, but I wrote that 'it will be an exceptional effort if we can get out of this game.' Jack Russell, meanwhile, had taken his 10th catch of the match to equal the world record for a Test. He celebrated with a cup of tea.

Day four

'Well,' I wrote, 'we're hanging on in there by the skin of our teeth. You've got to admire Athers. He's a strong, gutsy guy. He's still there on 82 and is an inspiration.' The captain had led us to 167 for four at the close, still a long way from survival but at least a tough response to an impossible chase. McMillan had earlier played his way to a hundred with South Africa batting on until he got there. I suppose they thought they had so much time to get us out that they could afford to do so. They eventually declared on 346 for nine just after McMillan reached his landmark, leaving us the best part of five sessions to survive or reach the highly unlikely target of 447 to win. I applaud them for letting McMillan get his hundred. I suppose with us subsequently batting for as long as we did, there must be question marks over the South African tactics, but at the time you could see why they were doing what they did. They seemed to have plenty of time. Jack took his 11th catch to break the record and this time was tempted into having a glass of champagne to celebrate. In his younger days Jack used to drink a fair bit, but he has gone completely the other way now and rarely touches a drop. I ended up with three for 84 off 29 overs, a lot better and figures that made me think that if only I'd got a couple of wickets in the first innings, I'd have been happy.

When we batted again with a mountain to climb, Mark Ramprakash got a duck, which put the lid on another disappointing spell for him in England colours. I could have cried for him. I wrote: 'He's got so much but he just can't do it at this level at the moment. Illy and Beefy [Ian Botham] both asked me what he was like in his preparations at home and I just told them that he's more relaxed at Middlesex, which obviously he is. But there's so much difference between a Test and a county game.'

Ramprakash was one of four wickets to fall before the close and we were left contemplating our chances of getting out of trouble. They weren't great. I felt we might get out of it, but that our biggest problem was that half the wickets left were the tail. Escapes in those sort of situations just don't happen very often. I'm sure people didn't turn up on the last day thinking, 'Here we go, we're going to lose,' but I'm also sure they wouldn't have dreamt we would save it. Yes, maybe we could make it last until teatime, but not what we did. It was truly incredible.

Day five

Michael Atherton played one of the great Test innings. Everybody said it. Raymond Illingworth said it and Ian Botham said it. I wrote: 'What a performance. You can't say enough about Athers. If you wanted two people to play for you in those circumstances, it would have been Atherton and Russell, but they exceeded all expectations. It's as good a feeling as a win.'

I can't describe what it was like sitting in the dressing-room that day at Johannesburg as Atherton and Russell repelled everything thrown at them to lead us to a draw, with only the wicket of Robin Smith falling all day. We all had sweaty palms and were looking at our watches every five minutes. This was pressure. It was worse for the people watching than for those in the middle. We didn't move for four hours. You could see the South Africans wilting as the day went on, because, after all, you can't keep on going all day in circumstances like that and not see your perform-ance suffer. South Africa must have been devastated. I felt they bowled too short. Atherton was dropped on 99 by Kirsten at short leg, a hard chance, but apart from that was immaculate in his 185.

There were some great scenes afterwards. Everyone wanted to give them a hug. Mike and Jack – who hung in there doggedly, too, for his 29 – were absolutely knack-ered, because they had thrown themselves completely into it. Robin was out, cutting to third man, in the morning, but we got through to lunch and then the longer it went on, the worse it got because it made me wonder how important my contribution with the bat might be. You tend to think that if you get in, as a tail-ender, before lunch, then it wouldn't really matter because you're going to lose and you wouldn't be expected to bat too long. But the pressure gradually builds up to a point where you batting for half an hour instead of 15 minutes could become very important. You get more and more nervous about it. Not that it ever got to the stage today where I had to put my pads on.

The relief at the end of it all was extraordinary. We were watching on television and people were saying, 'It's over, it's over.' I said, 'No, it's not, they're going to bowl another over.' Then we watched Hansie Cronje to see when he was going to go up to Atherton to shake his hand and say, 'Well done, we've had enough.' When he did, everyone, who had not been allowed to move from their positions while the stand evolved, sprinted out of the dressing-room onto the balcony. It was truly a great escape. We had all stayed where we were, only being allowed to go to the toilet during a drinks break or between overs, and even then only if we could guarantee we would be back in our positions by the resumption.

Ian Botham had told Mike that if he batted all day, they would drink the biggest bottle of cane between them they could find, and they duly did that later on. South Africa were very good about it, all coming in and shaking our hands. We had all bought diamonds in Kimberley and they were delivered to us that day, so we decided to give them to Robin Smith's dad for safe keeping at his home. Illingworth was worrying about this, asking if they would be in a safe. It was the last thing the rest of us were worried about after a game like that.

Later on, we went to a bar called Vertigo, about two miles from the hotel, and my cut-off point was 2am while most of the guys were still going strong. I was drunk and worn out so I went outside but couldn't get a cab. So I ran back to the hotel, through Johannesburg, shit-faced at 2.30am. I fell over two or three times and hit a couple of lampposts, but I made it. When I told someone what I'd done the next morning, they said, 'You shouldn't have done that. We might never have seen you again.'

Atherton had been a bit low during the game as it looked like slipping away from us, but now all that was

forgotten and he will struggle to ever surpass his achievement in this match. He is a quiet bloke, a bit of a loner in
many ways and quite happy to do his own thing and not be
surrounded by people all the time. I know him well, but I
still don't truly know what motivates him. He's not money-
orientated and he doesn't seem to be obsessed with passing
records. I just think he wants to be seen as a success as a
batsman and captain at the highest level.

He's very unselfish and always plays for the team. He's
also very determined, and different to what his background
might suggest. With an education at Manchester Grammar
School and Cambridge University, you might expect him to
be a bit of a jazz-hat, but actually there's no one harder or
gutsier to play against. The analogy used in 1997 by Steve
Waugh, when he likened Mike to a cockroach who keeps
on getting up when you stamp on him, is perfectly apt. He's
very dogged and doesn't want the kudos, the stardom or
the glory. He could have made so much more, in financial
terms, out of being England captain if he was that way
inclined, but he never bothers with many deals. He was just
determined to make England a successful side again.

Mike probably loves the game more than he lets on. I
think he likes the lifestyle the game gives him, likes the
people it enables him to mix with, and likes travelling and
playing the game in company with those people. He still
lives in a two-bedroomed flat in Didsbury that, the last time
I saw it, was a pigsty. He doesn't want material things.
There are no luxuries or trappings. He has an old wine-box
with his stereo on it in his room. He doesn't want much.

At one time I wondered whether Mike would carry on
playing county cricket when he finishes with England, but
now I think he will. He's had a harder ride than most

people but he's hung on in there and, if anything, has become more of an establishment figure now than when he first started and Lord's thought they were getting a classic university man. He's stubborn, to ridiculous levels at times, and he won't do what people expect of him just for the sake of it. That may have been what kept him in the England captaincy at the end of the 1997 Ashes series after he had twice offered to quit during the summer. But he was persuaded to change his mind by Lord MacLaurin. If he had gone then, he must have realised that would have been the end, he would never get another chance to captain England – so why not carry on and give it another go?

I thought he would go at the end of that season and he must have wondered at times why he stayed on in the job, but by staying he has also given the authorities more time to decide who's the best successor, and that can only be to the team's advantage. It reminded me of that time when we had a meal in Hampstead after the 'dirt in the pocket' Test and he was wondering whether to quit then. I told him that if he was happy that he had done nothing wrong and was happy with the way he conducted himself, then why jump? And I'm glad he didn't.

He tried very hard to make his relationship with Illingworth work. Mike still hasn't expressed his true feelings about the situation, but I don't think he had a lot of time for Illingworth. He had to make the best of it while it was happening and pretend that they could get on, but Mike had to bite his lip a great deal. Illingworth made him a scapegoat whenever something went wrong, but Mike just got on with it, which reveals just how much he must relish the captaincy, deep down.

He's certainly highly intelligent and very sharp. In

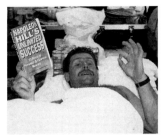

Both Devon Malcolm and Robin Smith were criticised by Ray Illingworth for getting distracted by other matters during the tour of South Africa in 1995–96. Smith's business interests were said to be a problem, but the book he was reading seemed to be an ironic comment on his duck at East London. (*Angus Fraser*)

Meeting Nelson Mandela was a highlight of the tour for all of us. (*Graham Chadwick/ Allsport*)

Devon Malcolm and Mrs Illingworth get together on the karaoke machine during the Christmas party. (*Angus Fraser*)

(*Above*) Mike Atherton and Jack Russell after their remarkable partnership in Johannesburg where they batted together for 277 minutes to save the match; Atherton's innings lasted for 643 minutes and was one of the great rescue acts of all time. (*Below*) Ian Botham presents Mike Atherton with a bottle of cane rum as a reward for his innings. (both *Angus Fraser*)

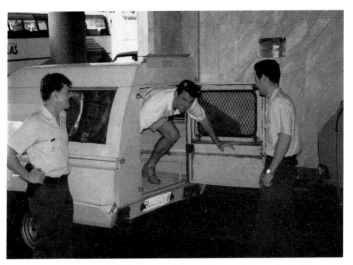

Physio Wayne Morton is finally let out of the security guards' van after he has been driven around Johannesburg 'under arrest'. (*Angus Fraser*)

Mike Atherton and I became great friends when we were both recovering from injury in the early 1990s. (*Angus Fraser*)

In action in Jamaica for the second warm-up game for the 1997–98 series in the West Indies. (*Lawrence Griffiths/Allsport*)

The relaid pitch at Sabina Park, Kingston, Jamaica. For the first time in Test match history the game was abandoned because the condition of the wicket was unsuitable for play. (*Clive Mason/Allsport*)

press conferences, he's able to quickly assess the question and calculate the best answers. He can come across poorly in them, but that's only when, to him, he's being asked meaningless and trivial questions. He is surly and dismissive when he thinks that the people who are writing and asking the questions should know full well what the answer is.

Mike is good company and good fun, contrary to the miserable image he sometimes gives out. He's thrilled when England win and satisfied with his own success. He knows he's a good player and he doesn't worry about what people say about him. He takes it more to heart when people criticise his captaincy rather than his technique, and he goes about his game in a studious way. You would always want him in your side, not only for his ability but for his inner strength. He looks opponents in the eye and takes them on, like he did Courtney Walsh in Jamaica.

He's so keen not to look soft that he can take his competitiveness a bit far, like being reluctant to clap opponents' fifties and hundreds, and will never yield to the public or agents who would like him to be a bit more upbeat. He is what he is and enjoys his life; there's nothing sad about him. Mike once told me a story that was typical of him, about when he went to pick up his OBE from the Queen. First he described how bored he was hanging around for it, and then told how he nearly got into trouble when he received it. He was supposed to walk backwards away from the Queen and then sideways, but he said he very nearly just turned away from her and walked off without remembering protocol. That would have gone down well!

Weaknesses? Well, he could give a player more notice

when he leaves them out, but he's not alone among England captains in being poor in this regard. I suppose there is so much going through their mind that they don't make it a top priority. He has struggled with certain aspects of the captaincy and could be a bit more sensitive to his players' frustrations at times, but his players are genuinely relaxed in his company. They are free to speak and act normally. Tactically, he's dropped me too often, so he can't be that good! But we've never fallen out over cricket. He feels it more than me when he drops me, because he's the 'bad guy' in the piece. He said to me recently that he thought he'd seen the last of me in an England team and didn't think I'd come back after South Africa.

But I know I'm back through merit. I know, despite some of the things that Illingworth has said, that I've never got in the team because Mike Atherton was my mate, or bowled at the right time because Mike Atherton was my mate. I've bowled and played when he has thought it is best for the team, it's as simple as that. And I'm glad about that; I don't want favouritism. We have an honest relationship where we can say what we feel. Sometimes I'll curse at him in front of the team and I have to say to myself, 'No, Gus, *you* might be able to say that to the captain, but it sets a bad example with young players around.' I was glad to play a few more Tests under his captaincy.

Mike was as happy as I've ever seen him that night in Johannesburg after his epic innings. The enormity of what he had achieved became more and more evident over the following few days. All of a sudden, everyone in South Africa knew him. I had a great day with him going round some superb vineyards in Paarl, but, all of a sudden, he became more distant towards me. I now think he must have

known that he was going to drop me from the Durban Test.
He duly did.

The interim

I was not the only one left out of the third Test. Devon
Malcolm and Darren Gough also found themselves on the
sidelines in a match that was once again ruined by the
weather. So we were still all-square, but my problem was
that there was not enough cricket for me to force my way
back in the side. I missed our match in Pietermaritzburg, so
I wasn't in contention for the fourth Test in Port Elizabeth,
which was a good match played in a magnificent atmosphere thanks to the efforts of the St George's band. Jason
Gallian had joined us from the A tour because of John
Crawley's serious hamstring injury, suffered in Durban,
and Gallian went straight into the side ahead of Ramprakash, who was now very low. I left him alone for a while
and then tried to have a comforting word with him, but it
was difficult to know what to say, even to a team-mate. I
knew how much talent he had and couldn't understand
why he struggled to produce it in Test cricket. It was really
sad.

This was also the time when the whole issue of having
our families with us on tour came to the fore. They had
arrived just before Christmas when we were preparing for
Port Elizabeth, and this time there were quite a few
children on the tour, because quite a few of us had had kids
at around the same time. To add to the numbers, a few
families brought nannies with them so that the wives, with
us not really being available to help with the kids, could
have a holiday, too.

Denise wasn't sure if she wanted to make this trip, but I talked her into it. My mum and dad wanted to come, too. When I first started playing, the temptation was to think it would last forever and that they could pick and choose their tours, but by now they realised they had to take the chance when they could if they wanted to watch their son playing cricket on tour for England. All of a sudden the tour party had increased to about 50 in number, and that takes a lot of organisation. Unfortunately, the management were not prepared to provide it. They knew how many people were coming, but on one occasion they tried to cram everybody into one coach and it ended up with a couple of players following on in a cab. Meanwhile, on the coach, some people were sitting in the aisle and there was tons of luggage accompanying us.

So I can see why England took the decision to exclude families from the following winter's tour to Zimbabwe and New Zealand. A mass of people had arrived with us in South Africa and the tour seemed to lose its direction. It was the worst it's been and I could understand the concerns of the management. But you need to see your family when you're away for a long time. You miss them dreadfully and I don't think it's purely coincidence that my best performances abroad have always coincided with family visits. John Crawley's diary from Zimbabwe, published in the *Sunday Telegraph*, received a lot of criticism, but it was clear he was missing his girlfriend and it's a delicate issue.

If I'm away for three months, I want to have the opportunity to see my children for at least a small part of that time. It's very expensive for us to fly our families out, but you have to be given the option. When I was young, my dad worked away for as long as 18 months at a time on occasions, but he was always allowed visits from us and to us, paid for by the company. Yes, it did become too much in South Africa – even though the sight of Mrs Shirley Illingworth and Devon Malcolm, drawn out of a hat together, doing a duet on karaoke night was one to savour – and it was chaotic at times, but management have the authority to control it. It was a stressful time for the players because they wanted to look after their families but also concentrate on the cricket. In Cape Town, we were in a hotel in a built-up area with no swimming pool, so clearly no thought went into the choice of that either. We were also warned of the dangers of walking around where the hotel was.

It's much easier in, say, Barbados, because there's no travelling involved and the families can simply leave at the end of the fourth Test, and I was glad to hear that the 'ban' had been lifted on families for my return tour to the West Indies. It backfired on the team to stop them coming to Zimbabwe and New Zealand, but there was reasoning behind why they did it. The solution is to cater for the families while they're with us and get the timing of the visits right. Again, the Australians, as with so many things, seem to get it right.

By the time we got to Cape Town for the final and decisive Test, Mark Ilott had got himself injured and we were looking to play four seamers, so there were two places up for grabs. That meant that Devon and I came in, having not played for almost a month, since the Johannesburg Test on 3 December. I had worked hard in the nets, but it's not the same as playing.

A further distraction going into the match was the announcement, on New Year's Eve, that I was not going to be kept on for the round of one-dayers that finished the tour in South Africa. I was in the initial party for the World Cup but, of that 18, I was the only one who was not required in South Africa, meaning that I would only be needed at the World Cup in an emergency. Seventeen stayed and I was sent home. I wondered what game the selectors had been watching. It really kicked the wind out of me at a time when I had to lift myself for a crucial Test I wasn't properly prepared for. I spent an hour or so on my own confirming, as if I needed to, that this was the most disappointing tour I'd ever been on. It had promised so much at the start, but it had been one let-down after another and it left me with an empty feeling.

It was left to Mike to tell me that I was going to miss out, but I wanted to hear why from Illingworth and I almost had to manufacture a situation where he was forced to have a word with me. Following a team meeting, I deliberately waited until the end so that only Raymond and I were left in the room and Wayne, who knew what was going on, took Mark Ilott for a drink so that I was left alone with Illingworth. Then he explained the decision and, while I didn't agree with it, at least it was nice to hear the reasons. I don't think he would have told me, though, if I hadn't forced the issue. For now, that had to be forgotten. The fifth Test was imminent.

Fifth Test, Newlands, Cape Town;
2–4 January 1996

Day one

If South Africa on the whole was a disappointment, Cape Town was everything I had been led to believe it would be. The scenery was stunning, Table Mountain was in the background and the vineyards were impressive. The perfect setting for the deciding Test.

The Newlands wicket was cracked and I thought it would deteriorate, but it had a bit of pace and bounce. We won the toss and batted very badly. Allan Donald bowled very well and we were dismissed for 153. Only 66 from Robin Smith gave us any sort of total. It should have been a good toss to win, but we didn't make the most of it. The ball seamed a bit at first but the wicket flattened out and our total was poor. Donald was quick and he hit me a couple of times but didn't get me out. Then Cork struck a couple of blows for us to have them 44 for two at the close and give us something to clutch at.

I bowled two innocuous overs and felt really nervous and under pressure. I bowled too short, but then I hadn't bowled for a month, so it was difficult. Devon was nothing like his best, either. He just tried to hit a length, but what England had were two bowlers who had been thrown into a Test with no match practice behind them; we were forced to try to find our feet in a big match, which was bloody difficult. I hadn't exactly frozen, but I stood at the top of my run up and felt, 'I'm not ready for this.' I had no confidence and I wasn't sure where the ball was going to go. You can bowl in the nets until the cows come home but it doesn't necessarily prepare you for a match. In a game, when you're hit for four you know it, whereas in the nets there's always the temptation to say, 'That would have gone to a fielder.'

Day two

On this morning, Atherton and Illingworth had made us all move into one dressing-room. There are two big ones for each side in Cape Town, next to each other, with a mutual sauna in the corridor. We were now up to 22 players, with the one-day specialists having arrived, and there was an enormous group of people present. The feeling was that people who were not involved in the match should not mix with those who were playing, and even though Mike was one of only four Test players in one of the rooms, he made the seven others lump all our gear into his one. I had got there early to get a good position and had found a nice comfortable corner. Next thing I knew, I had to move and ended up perched on the edge of a bench. When I asked Mike why the four hadn't moved in with the seven, he said: 'Well, does Mohammed go to the mountain?'

We worked so hard to get back in the match but it all fell apart with South Africa's last-wicket stand of 73. It was a hot, sweaty day, but I bowled much better from the start, even though my first over went for eight runs. At one stage I had figures of nought for 17 off three overs, but later it was one for 21 off 13 overs and I had bowled nine maidens in ten overs in the middle of an innings with an old ball. So I was hugely relieved about that. As it has turned out, this was my last Test match bowl for two years. It would not, if I hadn't been picked for the 1998 West Indies tour, have been too bad a way to bow out.

We had South Africa 171 for nine, only 18 ahead, and all we had to do was knock over the novice Paul Adams and we would be back in the match. Devon was brought back to do the job but he bowled slower than my pace and Adams put on a match-winning stand with David Richardson. When Devon first started bowling badly, a few of the guys began looking at each other as if to say, 'What was that, Dev?' but I was thinking, 'Give the bloke a chance, he hasn't bowled for a month.' All right, maybe he could have worked harder in the nets, but you just can't switch your form on and off. If I, who can bowl with as much control as most bowlers in the world, was forced to stand there wondering where the ball was going when I bowled, then someone like Devon Malcolm certainly wouldn't have known where it was going.

The nightmare last-wicket stand started when Adams got off the mark with a five. He went for a quick single, Cork had a shy at the stumps, the whole thing happened too quickly for anyone to back up and it went for four over-throws. Then Devon bowled a yorker that Adams somehow got an inside edge to and it went to fine leg, and then there were four leg-byes. Before we knew it, an over had cost 16 and our moment had gone. Adams continued to ride his luck and play well in equal measure, Richardson played very well and we could see the game slipping away. I came on near the end and immediately got Adams to miss a few, before Peter Martin returned and got him in his first over.

A lead of almost 90 shouldn't be enormous in the context of a Test, but from a position where we were to all intents and purposes level, they now had their noses in front and had gained the momentum. No one said very much after play about our failure to finish the job off – that was to come later – but we knew we were in trouble.

I had to change straight into my batting boots as I was

nightwatchman again – and I was in by the close, when Atherton was out. McMillan dropped me at slip off the very last ball of the day, which left me with the prospect of facing Donald again the next morning.

Day three
We were stuffed. We got rolled over again, this time for 157, and then they knocked off the 70 runs needed with the minimum of fuss. I didn't even get a bowl in their second innings. When you're 'the man', the ball is always being thrown at you; when you're not, you struggle to lay a hand on it. It was pretty deflating to stand there and not get on while so-and-so got a bowl.

There were a few contentious decisions when we batted. None more so than when Hansie Cronje was fined 50 per cent of his match fee for asking umpire David Orchard to use the third-umpire facility to judge on Graham Thorpe's run out. The umpire said it was not out, then the replay was seen by supporters in hospitality boxes and they started roaring that it was out. I don't think Cronje was unreasonable about it. He just went up to the umpire and said, 'Look, I'm sure you now realise that the decision was a lot closer than you first thought, so wouldn't you be better off using the third umpire?' So he did, and Thorpe was told he was out.

My view is that the third umpire should be used whenever possible and that we must use technology to get rid of as many mistakes as we can. With the coverage the game gets now, and the money involved, you must try to eliminate human error. I don't know why Cronje was fined so much, really – I suppose the International Cricket Council considered it to be questioning an umpire's decision, but I think that's ridiculous. OK, it worked against us on this occasion, but it was a perfectly reasonable request. Sometimes umpires are a bit stubborn, or think that they're better than they are and get a bit carefree. But decisions like that can change a match completely and I think umpire Orchard should be applauded for having had the courage to admit his mistake in time to be able to do something about it. Of course, Thorpe was unhappy about it and threw his bat in the dressing-room – he was told he wasn't out, then he was told he was. But if it had been the other way round, I would have been unhappy if it hadn't gone our way.

By the time South Africa batted again, we were a beaten team and so ended a disappointing series. I only took four wickets at around 45 apiece yet I bowled well in two of the three innings that I bowled in. But the final and perhaps biggest incident of the whole tour was still to come. We were standing out there for the presentations and listening to all the announcements telling us how great South Africa were, when the announcer said: 'We are pleased to announce that there will be an extra game on Saturday, a day-night match between England and Western Province.'

There was a mixture of reactions in our ranks. The players who had already been told that they weren't featuring in the one-day games said, 'Well, I'm not playing.' Then Atherton and Stewart went spare. There was thunder on their faces. It was: 'Who organised this? What's going on? We've had a bloody hard tour and need a couple of days' rest, not an extra game.'

We went into the dressing-room and asked what was going on. Illingworth said he had arranged it, so he and Atherton had a row over it, with Illy saying, 'The way some of you lot have been playing, you could do with an extra game. A lot of the stuff I saw out there was crap.' He then just carried on spouting off, while we were all dumb-founded. I honestly thought he was going to have a heart-attack; he was really red in the face and eventually had to go over to the basin and slap some water on his face and have a drink. Mike had had a go back at him and, before he finished, Illingworth turned to Devon, who was just sitting on the physio's table minding his own business, and said: 'And you've bowled shit, too.' We thought, 'Oh Christ, here we go. He had to single Devon out, didn't he?'

I wouldn't have been surprised if Devon had hit him. You could see his eyes changing as Illingworth laid into him. But he just started whistling while Illingworth was carrying on. Then, before he left, Illingworth said that he had seven players in the other room who were happy to play in the extra game and that he needed four more from us. He added that if he didn't get enough volunteers, he would get the players from somewhere else. Then he stormed out.

There was hush in the dressing-room as we all realised that something big had just happened. Then a voice from the corner, belonging to a senior England player who had better remain nameless, said, 'As soon as we get rid of that **** the better,' and everyone started laughing. Now, you want people to get emotionally involved, but not like that. Illingworth had lost control and had got personal. The tension between him and Devon had been high throughout the tour and this was the last straw. Yes, Devon had been inconsistent, but you can never accuse him of not trying. It's the way he is.

There are a lot of Christians in the South African

dressing-room and they don't really go out and party after a win. So they were quite reserved at the end of it all. A few of us just had a chat with some of their stronger characters over a drink and swapped some stuff. In the end, Illingworth got his volunteers, including Atherton and Stewart, who felt they should be seen to be in support of the extra match. And England were beaten.

Something else rather curious happened. At lunchtime on the third day, which turned out to be the final day, we were served a lasagne dish that was cold. It just hadn't been heated properly. It wasn't very nice but we were hungry and that was all we were going to get, so we ate it. Then, after the debacle, we arranged to meet as a team that night in a bar for a drink and a chat about where it had all gone wrong. But nobody made it, because we were all ill. Everyone who had eaten the lasagne was affected. Mike was the last one to fall ill and it didn't hit him until he was in a taxi going to the bar. He had to make a sudden stop and a hasty return to the hotel.

Then we got to thinking. At that stage, the fourth day of the match was expected to be the crucial one – and if it had been, we would all have been struggling to make it onto the field. On two occasions in the past, opponents of the South African rugby team have been taken ill the night before big games with food poisoning and have wondered whether they were sabotaged. I don't think we were, but it does make the mind boggle.

The aftermath

So ended a miserable tour. I had a few days in Cape Town with my family while the team prepared for the one-day series – which they lost convincingly – before leaving for home on 8 January. I'd always wanted to play in a World Cup, but I knew 1995–96 would be my last chance and that it was gone. I was selected in 1992 but was injured, and now I didn't make the final party for the tournament in India and Pakistan.

I was also thinking about my long-term future but by no means felt it was going to be the end for me at the top level, because I'd bowled well in the first innings at Cape Town. I certainly didn't think I'd have to wait as long as I did to get back, before being picked for my third tour of the West Indies.

David Lloyd took over as coach and must have had his own ideas. I also think there was a consensus among the management that I might have been a bit past it, so I didn't feature throughout 1996, nor in the tour of Zimbabwe and New Zealand or the Ashes summer of 1997. By the time the South African tour was over I'd had two or three years' non-stop cricket, so maybe there wasn't the edge to my game that there usually is. I felt I was fine, but perhaps my body didn't respond like it did at earlier times in my career.

Yet I always believed I would get back. To get the best out of myself in county cricket, I always need the carrot of England being there. I want to leave the game having achieved, or given myself the chance to achieve, as much as possible, and I need to get as much out of myself as I can. To think that I can still play for England makes me do that.

There have been times in the last few years when I haven't done very well – 1996 wasn't great, for instance. But I've still felt, on days when things have come off, that I've bowled better than most of the people around at the time and that I could still do a job for my country if thrown into it. You have to believe in yourself. When I started playing for England in 1989, I set myself the target of 200 Test wickets. I'd got 119 before the tour to West Indies in 1997–98, so I've still got a long way to go but the goal is still there. Meanwhile, I've seen so many players come in with the attitude of enjoying it while it lasts and making the most of the lifestyle in the short term. I've always wanted to be there long term.

England to South Africa 1995–96

First Test
Centurion Park, Centurion, 16, 17, 18, 19, 20 November
England 381 for 9 dec (G.A.Hick 141, M.A.Atherton 78, R.C.Russell 50 not out)
Result: Match drawn.

Second Test
The Wanderers, Johannesburg, 30 November, 1, 2, 3, 4 December
South Africa 332 (G.Kirsten 110, D.J.Cullinan 69, D.G.Cork 5 for 84) and 346 for 9 dec (B.M.McMillan 100 not out, D.J.Cullinan 61, J.N.Rhodes 57)
England 200 (R.A.Smith 52) and 351 for 5 (M.A.Atherton 185 not out)
Result: Match drawn.

Third Test
Kingsmead, Durban, 14, 15, 16, 17, 18 December
South Africa 225
England 152 for 5
Result: Match drawn.

Fourth Test
St George's Park, Port Elizabeth, 26, 27, 28, 29, 30 December
South Africa 428 (D.J.Cullinan 91, D.J.Richardson 84, G.Kirsten 51) and 162 for 9 dec (G.Kirsten 69)
England 263 (M.A.Atherton 72, G.A.Hick 62) and 189 for 3 (A.J.Stewart 81)
Result: Match drawn.

Fifth Test
Newlands, Cape Town, 2, 3, 4 January
England 153 (R.A.Smith 66, A.A.Donald 5 for 46) and 157 (G.P.Thorpe 59, S.M.Pollock 5 for 32)
South Africa 244 (D.J.Cullinan 62, D.J.Richardson 54 not out) and 70 for 0
Result: South Africa won by 10 wickets.

Angus Fraser's tour (1st, 2nd and 5th Tests):
Batting: 4 innings, 2 not out, high score 5 NO, runs 10, average 5.00.
Bowling: 66 overs, 21 maidens, 187 runs, 4 wickets, average 46.75, best 3–84.

england in west indies 1997–98

The background

I was pretty low when I left South Africa early in 1996. The tour had not gone well and I had only taken four wickets in three Test matches, admittedly only bowling in two of them. I got the feeling my face didn't fit any more. Ray Illingworth subsequently said that Mike Atherton had not become a real captain until he had dropped his mate (i.e. me) and I came back from that trip extremely worried about my international future.

There was a bit of a lifeline in that 17 players had been chosen for an initial World Cup squad and I was one of them but, as it turned out, 16 of the 17 went on to play one-day cricket during the rest of that winter and I was the odd one out. I arrived home after a few days in Cape Town with my family and watched the one-dayers on TV in which we got absolutely smashed – you don't get any satisfaction from sitting there watching that, but you do wonder if you might have made a difference. As it was we lost 6–1, hardly ideal preparation for the World Cup in India and Pakistan.

The only good thing to come out of my omission from the biggest one-day tournament in cricket was that I was then invited to do some commentary and summary work for Sky that I really enjoyed. It got me off and running as far as my television work was concerned. I used to watch cricket throughout the night with Charles Colvile and, in a way, that softened the blow of me not being there. I enjoyed it and I got to see how television coverage worked and how it was all put together. It hit home to me that television, as well as newspaper work, is one of the areas I want to get into when I finish playing and it is only when you do something like that that you realise how difficult it is and how good a job Charles Colvile does. Charles has his critics but he's brilliant at linking things together and when you have an ear piece in and can hear the chaos going on behind the scenes you appreciate that.

I was aware of some pains in my groin during my time in South Africa and I started doing fitness work straight away, because I was doubly determined to be fit for the start of the 1996 season to try to get back into the England side. This injury, however, hindered me and I went to see a specialist who recommended a Gilmour's groin operation to clear up the problem. That got it out of the way before the start of the season because it needed to be corrected.

Then 1996 was spent trying to force my way back into the England picture. I realised I could be quite a way away from selection because we'd been beaten by South Africa and other bowlers, like Cork and Martin, had had good tours and would start off the summer. Darren Gough had had a poor tour but he had youth on his side and Illingworth loved him, which helped. The selectors also seemed to want someone who was perceived to do more with the ball or who would give them more variety, so Alan Mullally came on to the scene after starting off the season strongly with Leicestershire. Alan went on to play nine successive Tests and did OK without really establishing himself.

As for me, I ended up taking 49 wickets for Middlesex in 1996. I didn't bowl rubbish, but maybe I didn't bowl as well as I can at times throughout the season and was a bit innocuous occasionally. I'd had a lot of cricket and there are times when you need a rest. The game can be hard for someone who is big like me and at this point in my career two years' non-stop cricket had knocked the stuffing out of me. Maybe I was in need of a rest to get the edge back into my game.

So I had to watch while England played India and Pakistan hoping I'd get a tour place at the end of the summer. Each Test I was sort of assessing the bowlers' performances and was having to cross off another potential comeback Test because they were doing OK. It never came and I had to put up with a not particularly memorable summer.

The only good thing to come, towards the end of the summer, was the award by Middlesex of a benefit for 1997, so time was then spent putting together a committee and hoping things would go well. I wasn't picked for the tour of Zimbabwe and New Zealand, so took the opportunity to go on holiday to Barbados, the first time we had really been away as a family since Alex was born.

That was to be a rare time for relaxation because the planning of the benefit took up a lot of time and 1997 then turned out to be the hardest year of my life. A benefit season is a wonderful opportunity for a cricketer but you end up rushing around like a lunatic all summer hoping people turn up to functions and that everything goes smoothly. I'm delighted to say it turned out to be a huge success and we made over £250,000, which is a phenomenal amount of money and I was very grateful to all those who helped make it possible.

There was also, of course, the small matter of trying to perform well on the cricket field and throughout the season it was actually a release to get out on the park and play because it seemed to be the only time I could get away from the telephone. The winter had not gone too well for England and some of the bowlers who had done well the previous summer had not excelled but others, of course, had pushed themselves forward. I just hoped my turn might come round again and that I would bowl well at the right times. The summer started fantastically well for England, when they won the first Test against Australia at Edgbaston, and I found myself, like the previous summer, crossing off the Tests for which I might be called up because, quite rightly, bowlers should have at least a couple of Tests to get things right. After Edgbaston there was no way things would be changed straight away and then there was a lot of rain at Lord's so my chances of a return grew slimmer and slimmer.

Meanwhile, though, I was bowling well. I took only 47 wickets that year, but I bowled better than that, and I just kept on working and working without getting the breaks. My name cropped up a couple of times in the England speculation and whenever I played against an England batsman they would tell me that I would have enjoyed bowling on the sort of wickets they were experiencing that summer. It was unusual for England, but for the first time I can remember our authorities were being urged to produce wickets to suit our strengths; and the groundsmen, on the whole, were responding. I would watch people like Glenn

McGrath and Paul Reiffel bowling on responsive wickets and realised that my type of bowling was back in fashion. I had a couple of chances to catch the selectors' eye but never took them and the crunch came when I faced the Australians for Middlesex. I bowled 35 overs, bowling OK, but got nought for 100 and must say I left Lord's after that one thinking that maybe England had passed me by and I had missed my last opportunity.

In my mind I had built it up as a big game and the Aussies were at their best, with the Waugh brothers playing superbly. I thought to myself, 'Perhaps I have kidded myself that I can still do it. Perhaps they've been right not to pick me.' It was a bad time. But then, towards the end of the season, I started taking a few wickets again and, with the selectors looking for more consistency, my name started cropping up as a candidate for the winter tour to the Caribbean. I remember playing golf with Mike Gatting after bowling well at Kidderminster and he was talking about the winter and who should go to the West Indies. I told him I thought I should go. I accepted that I wouldn't be in the starting line-up, but told him that I'd done well in the West Indies before and that there was no one else in the country with the experience to come in on tour and do a good job at short notice if someone was injured.

That was my reasoning. As a bloke to back up what they already had, then I was the best bet. The argument then began to gather momentum. I went to the Cricket Writers' Dinner and people were asking me a lot about my tour chances. I was on the *Sunday Telegraph* table with Mike Atherton, but I didn't ask him about it because I didn't want to hear the worst from the captain. Then I watched the NatWest Trophy final a couple of days before the party was picked when I saw Ashley Cowan take some wickets for Essex and thought 'I've had it now. That's sealed my fate.' But as it turned out both me and Ashley were picked.

The good news came from an unusual source. Sky TV had asked me to go into their studios to comment on the tour party whatever happened and I thought I might as well go – if I was picked it would be good fun, but if I wasn't I had to get on with the rest of my life so I might as well not hide. Then, on my way to Isleworth, the phone rang and a woman from Sky said: 'I haven't told you this but you've been picked.' The media had been alerted an hour early to prepare their bulletins and now I had been told too. Simon Dyson, my benefit chairman, then rang and told me because he had heard through his job with Associated Newspapers and I quickly rang Denise to tell her. I actually like savouring those moments on my own. I sat there in my car with a big smile on my face just thinking about things and congratulating myself. When there are other people around you don't really know what to say, but this time I could sit there shouting and punching the air!

You do set yourself a deadline when you are out of the England team, particularly at my age. You do think you've had your lot if that deadline comes and you still haven't forced your way back. I had said to myself that, realistically, if I hadn't been selected for this tour I may well have not come back. The recall arrived just in time. The wickets in the West Indies had always suited my bowling and I had a good record there. That the tour started in January was also in my favour, because I was able to complete my benefit season before I left and so began a hectic build-up. The fitness training was intense and I threw caution to the wind in doing a lot of running, an area I had virtually ignored since my hip injury. It was all good fun. I was like a kid with a new toy, so excited about being involved again and just overjoyed to be back. I couldn't wait to get started.

When I was picked there was a lot of talk about me also doing a bit of bowling coaching and David Graveney subsequently told me that he was sure it was something I would do automatically, but they had mentioned it to the press to emphasise the high regard they had for me. He said, 'Yes, we know you want to play and we want you to compete hard for a place, but we also want you to work with the other bowlers and pass on your experience.' I think it got written up a bit out of context. Coaching was never going to be my primary role, but it was almost as if Graveney had mentioned it to explain my inclusion because I suppose I was the nearest thing to a surprise selection.

It only involved little things, like having an early chat to Dean Headley, who had missed our win against Australia at The Oval in the last Test of the summer through injury. I basically told Dean that he should try to play whenever possible and should only drop out if he definitely couldn't make it. I said to him: 'For Christ's sake Dean, don't give a sucker an even chance. You're too honest. If it's touch and go between two players and you say you've got a slight injury then they'll leave you out and you might then have to watch the other bloke cement his place.' I then told him that if he gave me a sniff of a chance to grab his place then I was going to take it, and that there was a difference between pulling the wool over someone's eyes and gritting your teeth and playing through a niggle. Dean's a good bowler and we need him fit and firing.

Our indoor practices at Old Trafford were an eye-opener. We were handed some balls and told that they would be the ones we would use in the West Indies. I couldn't believe it because they had a prominent seam, like the ones we used in England in 1989, and moved sideways in the nets. So much so that the batsmen couldn't lay a bat on them and we had to go back to the old balls so that they could get some decent practice. Again, I was trying to make an impression before we went and I actually bowled better than anybody else at practice. Around this time I also played golf with Mike Atherton and he had said, winding me up as usual: 'Have you seen the itinerary? You'll be carrying the drinks a lot out there.' To which I replied, 'No I won't. I'll be playing. I'll force my way in. You'll see.'

I didn't know, however, that it would be at the expense of an injured bowler. During training Darren Gough would make the odd negative comment about his fitness, but I just thought it was Goughy being Goughy and over-dramatising everything until I heard, one morning by switching on Ceefax, that he'd had to pull out with knee and hamstring problems. That changed everything for me. From being a back-up I was now almost certain to play because the selectors were unlikely to take a gamble on the inexperience of Ashley Cowan or Darren's replacement Chris Silverwood early on. The ball was in my court. I had a chance to re-establish myself but I didn't feel under any extra pressure. My chance had come.

The build-up

The tour, my third to the West Indies, could not have got off to a more soggy start. We were due to spend a week at the Club Antigua complex at the new, impressive training ground that had been built there, but so bad was the weather that we had to make an early departure for Jamaica in an attempt to gain some practice. I think swapping the paradise setting of Antigua for more time in Kingston, Jamaica, emphasised our commitment to the job in hand!

It was definitely the right decision. We based ourselves at the Kensington Cricket Club in Kingston and were spoilt rotten there by being handed excellent practice facilities and wickets. We really did have good sessions there getting used to the heat and humidity.

The worst time for me in the build-up to the Test series was undoubtedly the news that Denise's father had died. He had been ill for some time and it was felt by everyone that I was better off staying where I was rather than flying home, because there was a limit to what I could do at home and thankfully Denise was surrounded by her family. It was an unsettling time but I was grateful for Denise's support in encouraging me to stay on the tour and reassured by the knowledge that she had strength in numbers at home.

We then went up to Montego Bay for our first warm-up game, where we were faced with a hazardous pitch, which was, unfortunately, a sign of things to come. Not, though, my performance on it, for I failed to take a wicket in our comfortable win against Jamaica and instead 'distinguished' myself by fielding at back stop to cover for Jack Russell because of the uneven bounce, a position I feel, having enjoyed appealing for LBWs along with the slips, that I could make my own!

It helps to have a laugh about that game because the

truth of the matter was that it was a nightmare for me. I was rubbish. I was, admittedly, a bit nervous and struggled for any sort of rhythm, but while I was finding it all hard work, Caddick, Headley and Tufnell were excelling and did all the bowling as we won the game. I had time to do a lot of thinking, down there at long stop, and again many negative thoughts entered my head. I wondered if I'd kidded myself that I could still do it; I wondered if I was going to make a fool of myself in the series and would be announcing my international retirement before the winter was out. In practice I had looked good, but all of a sudden I was in a match and I had to perform. Until I had performed I couldn't convince myself that I was still able to do the job.

When the match finished, with me wicketless, I was still desperate to find some form so I asked if I could go out onto the Montego Bay pitch and have a bowl from the end where it had all happened for the bowlers, just to try to make it happen for me. So Wayne Morton, our physio, came out with a baseball mitt and John Emburey, the bowling coach, watched me go through the motions. Nothing seemed wrong, perhaps it was just the pressure which comes from bowling in an England shirt again, but I was worried about my future.

But then came a more conventional surface at Chedwin Park, Kingston, on which I did get among the wickets against West Indies A to confirm my place in our team for the first Test at Sabina Park. Ashley Cowan was also picked for Chedwin Park, which made me acutely aware that my Test place was not automatic, and that if Ashley had bowled well in this one I was struggling and he would play in front of me. Nothing was said to me but you just get vibes and feelings. People sort of take a step backwards from you, as if you're not a proper part of things any more. After a while you just sense you're under pressure but, thankfully for me, the complete opposite of Montego Bay happened.

I slipped into a rhythm straight away and the ball came out just right. I got a couple of early wickets and I was off and running. I kept going and ended up with five wickets on a flat surface. The doubts had instantly gone. I thought, 'I'm OK. I can still do it. Why the hell was I thinking the way I was? Why did I doubt myself?' You end up talking yourself up in the same way that you'd talked yourself down! My mood had improved considerably, not least because of the humour of the announcer at Chedwin Park, who was in the habit of reading out a player's career statistics as he came out to bat or bowl. When it came to Ashley, he simply said, 'As the song said, he ain't done nothing yet . . .'

Fairly routine tour stuff, then, up to now, apart from the attention handed out to Dean Headley, grandson of the legendary Jamaican George Headley and greeted by us with a chorus of 'Headley's coming home', to the tune of 'Three Lions' by the Lightning Seeds on our arrival in Jamaica. 'I don't want to make a fuss about all this,' said Dean as we came through customs. Then he proceeded to talk to about three-quarters of the local population about his heritage within a day of getting there!

Routine, that is, except that the first Test lasted just 10.1 overs before it was abandoned because of an even more dangerous pitch than Montego Bay, the first Test in history to finish in such a premature and highly unsatis-factory way.

We had been aware that the Sabina pitch had been relaid, part of the West Indies' policy of trying to bring a bit more life back to their surfaces after a boring series against India in 1997. But this was something else. We had a glimpse of it when Jamaica played Barbados on the Test pitch soon after we arrived on the island and you could see straight away that it wasn't flat. When a group of us went for a walk round the ground during that Jamaica match, I was also quickly reminded of the cricket-loving locals' sense of humour. Some bloke up in the scoreboard shouted out to me 'Fraser'.

'Yes?'

'You look like an old cow to me – full of runs!'

At least the stick in the West Indies is jovial, unlike that you can receive from the crowds in Australia and South Africa.

The batsmen were concerned going into the game, but we took the decision that it could only get lower and more uneven so we decided we would be better off batting first when Mike Atherton won the toss. We were without Russell, who was taken ill the night before the game, remarkable for a man who is so careful over what he eats. But we were in good spirits as we settled down to watch Athers clip the first ball of the game off his legs for two. Soon after, however, balls started flying from nowhere and there was a sort of collective 'Christ, hang on a minute! What's going on?'

When Atherton was out trying to leave one, poor Mark Butcher, who had come in at the last minute for Jack despite not having played up to that point on tour, got an unplayable delivery first ball and came back to the dressing-room in a state of disbelief. After we had all watched the replay, though, we could reassure Mark that no one in the world could have played that ball and our batsmen were soon scurrying in every direction trying to find as much protective equipment as possible. Phil Tufnell, meanwhile, was looking for the biggest chest protector he could find.

I couldn't watch by this stage and just got my head down in a corner of the dressing-room and it was when Nasser Hussain was out for one that it began to dawn on us that this was something out of the ordinary. Nasser came and said: 'The umpires have got to show some balls here and call this off. You just can't play on that.' Atherton, who handled the situation superbly, was quickly taking the initiative and talking to match referee Barry Jarman, and then, when he was summoned onto the field by Alec Stewart, Brian Lara and the umpires, Steve Bucknor and Venkat.

It wasn't a surprise when it was eventually called off. When the game becomes a lottery like that it was the only real option and the West Indies realised that too. There were no complaints from their bowlers, Courtney Walsh and Curtly Ambrose. It's interesting to observe our people in that situation. I can honestly say that I don't think anybody was worried about physical injury. They were just wondering how on earth they could play on that surface. Phil Tufnell said that, if he had had to bat, he would have taken guard, left his bat standing in one of the huge cracks on the surface and walked away, hoping that any ball he received would hit it!

Then Stewart brought the house down in the press conference when he said, in a reference to a much-publicised case involving Geoff Boycott, that if he had stayed out there much longer he would have had as many bruises as a certain lady in a French court!

The possibility of back-to-back Tests in Trinidad was soon raised and one of the younger members of our party said: 'What's the wicket like there?' The reply from a more seasoned campaigner was instant. 'Well, we scored 46 last time!'

But off to Port-of-Spain we went, a ten-hour journey from Jamaica and a hastily arranged practice match was organised to get us ready for the 'start' of the series. The figures from the aborted Sabina affair, meanwhile, will still officially count in Test records, a decision welcomed by Stewart who finished on a hard-earned nine not out, but not exactly designed to bring a smile to the faces of Butcher and Hussain. As for me, I think it's right that they should stand even though, with a second Test in which I haven't bowled a ball now on my record, my strike rate has not exactly been enhanced.

The Jamaicans were devastated about what had happened. They did all they possibly could to make it up to the English holidaymakers who had had their trip of a lifetime ruined. Some people said that if it had been the other way round and the West Indies had batted first then it would have been a different story, but that's disappointing because all the West Indian players knew what the story was. Both Walsh and Ambrose knew the match should never have been played. They didn't get any satisfaction from those few overs of play. There wasn't a person there who didn't know that and we will never know if the same thing would have happened if they had batted first. But Caddick and Headley can be as quick as their bowlers so I'm sure it would have been equally as dangerous – the only uncertainty is whether

Lara would have wanted to end it because he would have been under a lot of pressure from the home authorities to bat on.

What I do know is that we got a lot of unfair stick from the locals and were even advised not to go and watch Jamaica play an international football match in Kingston in case we were recognised.

Second Test, Queen's Park Oval, Port-of-Spain, Trinidad; 5–9 February 1998

Day one

I was nervous when we took the field in Trinidad. After the Jamaican debacle I needed to get out there and get going in Test cricket again. We knew it would be a low-scoring affair again as the pitch was well grassed but it was never going to be as bad as Sabina. So it was particularly nice to contribute with the bat as I hung around for an hour, scoring 17 runs, in company with Hussain, getting hit on the head twice but living to fight the second day as we reached 214, a competitive score in the circumstances.

Day two

I don't think I touched the ball which ended my little bit of defiance with the bat, but as I had played and missed about 30 times and been hit all over my body I think I can say, as a member of the bowlers' union, that the West Indies deserved my wicket! When my turn came to bowl all sorts of things were going round my head. I was wondering if I still had it. I was thinking of those who still questioned me. My first ball back was to Lara – there are other players in the world I would rather have been welcomed back by – and I soon had an edge that didn't carry, which made me wonder if Test cricket was about to tease me again.

But things began to go my way. I thought that I had bowled better than this but I was grateful to take anything that went my way. Stuart Williams played a poor shot to me to get me off and running and things went from there. I got Lara, which was the wicket that took me past Ray

Illingworth's total of Test victims – caught Atherton, bowled Fraser. Perfect.

It got better. I had five wickets by the end of the second day and we were looking at a first-innings lead on a pitch that we were sure would be hardest to bat on last. I couldn't believe it had happened. I couldn't be more happy. My figures stood at 13–1–47–5. Perhaps I had bowled too many four-balls and I had certainly bowled better but I willingly settled for that. I'm perfectly happy to have a few unlucky days with Middlesex and get all my good luck in Test matches! I rang Denise to discover that she had not seen too much of the action because my son, Alex, had preferred to watch Power Rangers than his dad's comeback! But even I didn't expect to wrap things up quite so quickly on the third morning.

Day three

Conditions were not easy. I have talked earlier about the heat and humidity of Trinidad and the week of our Test was hot, even by local standards. It was like a microwave oven inside your whites. I felt like my skin was on fire. But I am fit and that helped me get through. I took all three of the remaining home wickets to beat my own record for the best figures by an Englishman against the West Indies. Not that it was sealed in classical circumstances. I gained a caught and bowled off Ambrose with what some people felt was a cunningly disguised slower ball. But what actually happened was that I got my run-up wrong and the ball just sort of fell out of my hand. I was almost embarrassed rather than euphoric. I felt as though I should apologise to Curtly.

In some respects I didn't realise what I had achieved. I

bowled better in Barbados in 1994. I actually bowled better in the second, ill-fated, innings of this match. And in the middle of a hard-fought, tense match, I was in no mood to celebrate. I thought 'I'll enjoy it at the end.' Yet it was destined to be spoilt. For now I took receipt of a lovely number of congratulatory faxes and a bottle of champagne sent by the *Sunday Telegraph*. Our blokes batted bloody well at the start of our second innings and, at the close on the third day, 242 ahead with six second innings wickets remaining, we were in an enviable position. I went out for dinner with a group of people including Ian Botham and it was strange sitting next to the great man and having him congratulate me on a performance. I was also congratulated by Geoff Boycott, who had laid into me in print at the start of the tour. I wrote in my diary 'the two-faced git'.

Day four
True, Curtly, who was supposed to be over the hill, bowled extremely well to blow our second innings away on the fourth morning. But the West Indies still had to get 282 to win the game on a worn and still uneven pitch. They had their luck but we let them get the runs, somehow.

Some people have asked whether I should have got the new ball in the second innings after my 'eight-for' but I'm perfectly happy to be first change. And I got three more wickets, including Lara again, as they slipped to 124 for five, to reach 10 in a Test for the first time. It should have been game over.

Then, however, came David Williams and Carl Hooper. They hung on in there until the close, leaving the West Indies with a hundred to get and five wickets in hand. Then came the moment that will haunt me.

Day five

From the very first ball of the final day, Williams hit a return catch back to me that seven times out of ten I would have claimed gratefully. But it went down. 'I hope that's not another Chanderpaul,' I said to myself, thinking back to the Trinidad Test of 1994 when Graeme Hick put down Shivnarine Chanderpaul with us in a winning position and we went downhill from there. I went from hero to villain in the space of one ball. Then I had to think about getting back to business.

I felt I had Williams LBW after that, and three times in all, and then Jack dropped him off me, a difficult leg-side chance. It was all going wrong. By this time my exertions were catching up with me. The legs still felt fine, but I was almost lethargic and I couldn't make an impact with the second new ball.

Our fortunes were summed up when I bowled a ball to Kenny Benjamin after Williams was finally out that went along the ground, just missed the off stump and went through Jack to hit the helmet behind him. Five byes that put the lid on our chances and soon after the West Indies had clinched a famous victory.

I must say that Carl Hooper was magnificent for his unbeaten 94. He deserved to get the Man of the Match award ahead of me. But it did little to make it easier for us. We were desolate afterwards, in that same dressing room as we had to sit after being dismissed for 46 four years ago and our rain-ruined draw in 1990. Athers sat with his head in a towel and nobody spoke. A few of us went into the West Indies dressing-room to congratulate them and then we went our own ways in the evening when I had a few too many drinks.

I was proud about my performance but I was also empty. I have claimed all three balls used by us and one day, when the pain has eased, I will look back in satisfaction. Did I feel let down by the other bowlers? No way! I am as aware as anyone that bowlers don't get it right every game. Tuffers bowled pretty well, even though he did continually come over the wicket, but Dean Headley and Andrew Caddick had poor matches by their standards. It happens. Other people will carry me at other times, I'm certain of that, so I must just be grateful for my wickets while feeling totally deflated that they have come in a losing cause.

It was so distressing at the end. We got drunk that night and by the end of a miserable day there was Athers, in a terrible state, having a go at Brian Lara, half in jest. Three times I had played at Trinidad and three times I had been robbed. The first one, in 1990, was a draw and the second one we lost after being in a winning position. This time we had just thrown it all away.

The interim

We had to concentrate on the positives from Trinidad with another Test following so quickly. It was encouraging that we had played as well as we had and outplayed them for a long period of time. I've played when we've been totally hammered and you struggle to take anything positive from it, but this was a close game that could have gone either way and we'd competed well. It made us realise that if we played as well as we could then we could beat the West Indies. The bottom line, though, was that having worked so hard and done so much right we had still lost. There was no getting away from that.

It was time for David Lloyd, our coach, to lift everybody and this he did. There was criticism, too, mainly for Caddick and Headley, who had not bowled as well as they can in the West Indies' second innings. That did not go down well with Andy, who is an intriguing character and well worth looking at in more detail. Andrew Caddick is essentially quite shy and not the most confident person in the world but by trying to look confident he can rub people up the wrong way. He's got a heart of gold and there's nothing he wouldn't do for any member of the side, but he can be abrasive which might have something to do with coming from a different background to us. He grew up in New Zealand and, really, is from a different culture.

Andy's wife lovingly calls him Britannica, after the encyclopedia, because there isn't a subject he doesn't know something about, and variations of that theme have seen him dubbed Ceefax and Handy Andy, but he has his uses and does seem to know how to fix things and do things that other people can't. If there's a problem, like if the television in the dressing-room has gone wrong, he will be the first one up there looking at it and fiddling with something or another. He's always saying 'I know what I'm doing.'

But Caddick is not a loner, as he's often portrayed to be. He can annoy people and he is reluctant to admit he's wrong, but he likes company and essentially the players like him. There was a great story I can tell about Caddick which happened during the final Test in Antigua during a break for rain and summed up what the man is like. Our bowlers were sitting down talking about seaming the ball, because Ambrose had been nipping the ball back to Alec Stewart on the first day of the match but then moving it away from him on the second. We were talking about whether bowlers in general, and Ambrose in particular, could control seam movement, as opposed to swing, and the general consensus among us was that even he couldn't and he was just trying to get it to move. But Andy said that he could control seam movement nine times out of ten.

We didn't believe it, but he insisted he could do this so I wandered over to the other side of the dressing-room, where Ambrose and Walsh were sitting, and I said, 'Excuse me Amby, we've been having a discussion after watching you bowl this morning and we wondered if you knew which way the ball's going to go because there's someone at our end who reckons he can control seam movement.' He replied that he couldn't, he was just trying to hit a good length and nip the ball away but sometimes it nipped in, which was not the end of the world.

'Why? Who thinks he can do that?'

'Guess?'

He immediately said, 'Caddick.'

When I confirmed the identity of our man, Curtly just grinned and said: 'Well, can you send him down here so he can show us how to do it when he's got a spare moment!' There were two bowlers with 300 Test wickets apiece asking for Caddick to show them how to do something!

I went back and Caddick was furious, saying I'd made him look a fool but he still wouldn't admit that it is impossible to be sure which way the ball will seam. Then, when the West Indies batted, we were getting smashed everywhere by Philo Wallace and Clayton Lambert and I had to keep going from fine leg to fine leg for the left and right handers. When I moved in front of the home dressing-room Ambrose poked his head out of the door, after Caddick had gone for 15 in an over, and said, with a big smile on his face, 'God knows what would happen if he didn't know what he was going to do with it!'

Andy Caddick can be a frustrating bowler to watch. He's got everything. Pace, bounce and movement and, on his day, I see him bowl and wish I had what he's got. I've got certain qualities but he gets more out of a pitch far more easily than I. When he gets it right it moves away and carries to the keeper and he's truly world class. But he doesn't get it right, at Test level, as often as he should do and I don't know why that is. Sometimes, when you've got too much up your sleeve, you can find yourself with five options for every ball and you're not sure what to do with it. If you've got less up your sleeve you have fewer alternatives. So whereas I tend to say to myself 'Shall I bowl a yorker? No, it could come out as a half-volley or a full toss, sod it', Andy would try it. When it comes off it's brilliant but there are very few bowlers who can bowl everything that well and sometimes he tries too much.

He struggles sometimes as his natural length, on slower wickets, can be fractionally short and batsmen can look to pull him. When that happens, like most bowlers, you then try to pitch it on a fuller length and over-compensate. If he's hit off his length he struggles to get it back, which is maybe why he's not done as well as he might have done yet. Is Andy mentally weak under pressure? I have heard that said in the media, but he took five wickets in really tense circumstances against Australia at The Oval in the last Test of 1997 so I'm not sure about that. It's just that talent is making the most of what you've got and, at the time of writing, Andy Caddick, unfortunately, isn't doing that. He should be as good a bowler as Glenn McGrath, if not better because he moves it away more. Given the way he came back from a serious shin injury, he must have character and determination. Hopefully, for England's sake as well as his own, he will come back again.

Third Test, Queen's Park Oval, Port-of-Spain, Trinidad; 13–16 February 1998

Day one

The pitch was a bit better for this Test, obviously because the groundsman had been preparing it for longer. We had had two days off and just tried to think positively. I had to crank my body up again because back-to-back Tests can be really tough. I had had a word with both Dean and Andy reminding them that they were good bowlers, and Ian Botham appeared in the nets to offer his encouragement too, which was nice. And the first day went really well for us.

We put them in, which I wasn't sure was the right decision, but we got out of jail by bowling well on a day when they batted badly. My good luck carried on and I wrote in my diary 'long may it continue!' I took another five wickets to complete 10 five-wicket hauls in Test cricket, one of my goals achieved. I slipped into a good rhythm, as did Andy which was equally pleasing, and the West Indies tried to do things too quickly. As it turned out they were bowled out for 159 but we lost two wickets before the close.

Day two

This was a pretty ordinary day with the bat for us. I wrote, 'To be dismissed for 145 is disappointing. We've got to make them work harder for our wickets than this.' As usual we had made it hard for ourselves – is there such a thing as a boring Test involving England? We were back in the fray by the close and thankfully my body felt OK even if I wanted a longer rest.

Day three

This was another day of hard work for the seamers but collectively we did superbly well to dismiss the West Indies cheaply again, this time for 210, to give us a fantastic chance of victory. I was absolutely shattered by the end of the day. Utterly out on my feet. Jimmy Adams hung around but he eventually drilled one to Athers at mid-off and we were chasing a target.

This was the make-or-break day of our series, the day when we could lose everything. We had to deliver and we did. Every bowler contributed. Dean bowled magnificently for two and a half hours without reward before finally getting among the wickets and I got Lara out again, for the fourth time out of four on this tour, on my way to four for 40 and another nine wickets in the match and 20 in the two Trinidad Tests. Dream stuff! The only downside of snaring the main man again was that the *Sunday Telegraph* asked me to do an article on my secret for dismissing Lara – of course I failed to get him again all series! This time, the Australian umpire, Darrell Hair, correctly gave Lara out LBW but then sidled up to me, with a smile on his face, and said, 'Gus, how can I get off of this island alive?' We were 52 without loss at the close, chasing 225 to win, and an agonising couple of days were ahead of us.

Day four

This was another day of torture with me sat in the same corner of the dressing-room with my stomach in knots. I didn't want to move in case a wicket fell when I did. I just couldn't watch a ball live. It's funny how superstitious you can get. We had worked ourselves into a good position but we were on and off for rain and the match dragged on to the point where, at the close, we needed 38 to win with six wickets left and I wrote in my diary, 'This should be a doddle, but in a Test in Trinidad anything can happen. We need to be confident. Yes, we will win. Only now can I start thinking about my own success. I've had little chance so far but I just want the game to finish in our favour. As it is I've got another night of tossing and turning.'

Day five
We had to reach the highest score of the match to win, but we did it. What a nerve-racking experience. The atmosphere in the dressing-room was as tense as I have ever experienced but to come through eventually with Butcher and Headley at the crease was incredible. I didn't watch a ball, again, until we were seven wickets down but lunch came at an awkward time for us. We just wanted to get the whole thing over with, but Walsh and Ambrose bowled all day and Mark said that he had never batted so long without receiving a bad ball to hit. All through the series these two great fast bowlers kept on proving that they still had what it takes. At the end of this one it was more a feeling of relief than excitement. The pressure was great and four months of hard work were on the line. Some of us, including me, were quite emotional at the end. Their players came into our dressing-room which was nice and then the celebrations continued around the pool when we returned to our hotel with champagne and food everywhere. All the England supporters were clapping as we walked past them and even Lord MacLaurin, the chairman of the England and Wales Cricket Board, was thrown in the pool.

We spent the afternoon talking and drinking rum before, in the evening, we were invited to Lara's new house which was a magnificent building in a great location. It was almost palatial. Mike Atherton's two-bedroomed flat in Didsbury this was not. Actually, it was a bit ostentatious for my liking but Lara jokingly told me he'd named one of the bedrooms after me for the part I played in getting it built, having been one of the five England bowlers who played in the match at Antigua in which he set the world Test batting record in 1994. The other rooms were called the Caddick, Lewis, Tufnell and Hick suites!

The evening made me realise the pressure Lara is under. Everywhere he goes people want to talk cricket with him. We all eventually went back to the Pelican, our Trinidadian watering hole, where Atherton and Lara continued their 'play fights'. This time Athers had Brian in a headlock and some of the boys reckoned he was building up to pulling a knife on him by the end of the series.

The aftermath

At 1–1, between two evenly matched sides, there was all to play for but as so often with England it had gone wrong by the end of the series. We lost two important tosses, in Guyana and Antigua, and in the first of those matches we were outplayed. We played two spinners, which I felt was a basic error because it left the bulk of the seam bowling to me and Dean in extremely hot conditions. My solution would have been to ask Alec Stewart to keep, but as it turned out it probably would not have made much difference.

Barbados saw the arrival of our families, which was great, and also the arrival of a new pair of West Indian opening batsmen, Philo Wallace and Clayton Lambert. All along David Lloyd had said that he hoped these two would play because our suspicion was they were little more than sloggers, but how they proved us wrong. They really launched into the bowling with an elan rarely seen in Test cricket.

We had the better of the match and the highlight of both the Test and, as far as I'm concerned, the whole tour was the sight of Mark Ramprakash scoring his maiden Test hundred. To see his face light up after reaching three figures was something else. I knew how good a player Mark was and to see him struggle to do himself justice in Test cricket over the years was painful. He had done well in Guyana and now he played a truly great innings. We were in the driving seat going into the last day but then the rain came. The moment you want a nice clear day it pours down. True, the West Indies had a bit of a chance too but we were confident that if anyone was going to win that match it would have been us. But it was not to be.

Antigua was another important toss lost by us on a damp wicket which was dangerous early on. We were rolled over cheaply, and Wallace and Lambert fired along at six and seven an over before our last-day defiance was spoilt when the run-out of century-maker Nasser Hussain was followed by one of our spectacular collapses. A 3–1 defeat looks like a pasting but the series was much closer than that.

The series ended on the saddest possible note. I got the impression, in between the last two Tests, that Mike Atherton was about to resign as captain. He'd told me he wasn't sure if he was going to carry on or not and he was concerned about taking over the leadership of the one-day side from Adam Hollioake, who had led a successful trip to Sharjah. Then we were all lined up for the presentation ceremony at the St John's Recreation Ground when Athers asked if he could have everybody in the dressing-room for two minutes after the presentation. I knew then he was going.

Myself and Nasser were in tears in the dressing-room when he broke the news. Mike thanked everybody for their support over the last four years and said he was stepping down. That was that. Then he went out to face the press and we all just sat there, numb, without saying a word. I then packed my bags and swapped a shirt with Ambrose. Then an emotional night was spent back in the hotel complex.

So much was on my mind. It was a devastating way to finish a Test series of such promise, but I could look back on it with pride. I was back in business. I want to be as high on the all-time wicket-takers list as possible and I had taken 27 in this series, the equal of John Snow's record against the West Indies, and I had also become the all-time leading overseas wicket-taker in the Caribbean. Then there was the added advantage of doing well in the one-day internationals I played in which opened the door for me again as a one-day player.

During the first match of the 1998 tour of the West Indies I was wondering if I had lost what it takes to be an international bowler. By the end I was equalling a record and was as secure as you can be in the England side. I hope I can remain there for a couple of years yet.

Having taken more than 20 wickets in a series for England for the first time, and after 11 previously unsuccessful attempts in nine years, you would be right to think that I returned to the UK from the Caribbean full of confidence and really looking forward to taking on South Africa. By beating them 2–1 in an enthralling summer's cricket, this series not only provided me with the highlight of my career to date, namely a series win against a major Test-playing nation, but also another 24 wickets too.

Even to those playing, this victory seemed highly unlikely on the Saturday of the third Test at Old Trafford as we stared down the barrel of an innings defeat. However, through sheer determination in that match and then by putting in two fine performances at Trent Bridge and Headingley we managed to win our first five-match series since 1986–87.

The winter of 1998–99 gave us the opportunity to try to repeat this feat and, despite losing to Sri Lanka in a one-off Test at The Oval, we left for Australia realising the size of the task ahead but fancying our chances of bringing the Ashes back home to England. These hopes failed to materialise as we were outplayed and well beaten by a superior Australian outfit. This was a huge disappointment to us, as we failed to maintain the standards we set ourselves last summer.

Personally the tour was also a disappointment as I failed to make anywhere near the sort of impact I would have liked. On the field I didn't fire, I didn't feel I bowled as badly as my figures suggested, however I didn't create anywhere near the pressure or chances I expected. I must say though the way I was treated by the selectors did me no favours at all. Seldom in my ten-year international career to date have I ever felt I was an automatic choice for the England team, but having taken 56 Test wickets in a calendar year and made significant contributions in each of our wins in 1998 I found it hard to accept and understand when I was dropped for the second Test at Perth.

Even though on the field the year ended on something of a low for me I shouldn't complain. Taking 58 wickets at 22.88, followed by an MBE in the New Year's honours list for services to cricket, an award I was absolutely chuffed to accept, makes it a great year. So during 1998 I have once again gone full circle, it is now up to me to dust myself down pick up the pieces and prove the buggers wrong again in 1999. Here goes.

England to the West Indies 1997–98

First Test
Sabina Park, Kingston, Jamaica, 29 January
England 17 for 3
Result: Match abandoned.

Second Test
Queen's Park Oval, Port-of-Spain, Trinidad, 5, 6, 7, 8, 9 February
England 214 (N.Hussain 61 not out, A.J.Stewart 50) and 258 (A.J.Stewart
73, C.E.L.Ambrose 5 for 52)
West Indies 191 (B.C.Lara 55, A.R.C.Fraser 8 for 53) and 282 for 7
(C.L.Hooper 94 not out, D.Williams 65, S.C.Williams 62)
Result: West Indies won by 3 wickets.

Third Test
Queen's Park Oval, Port-of-Spain, Trinidad, 13, 14, 15, 16 February
West Indies 159 (A.R.C.Fraser 5 for 40, A.R.Caddick 5 for 67) and 210
(J.C.Adams 53)
England 145 (C.E.L.Ambrose 5 for 25) and 225 for 7 (A.J.Stewart 83)
Result: England won by 3 wickets.

Fourth Test
Bourda, Georgetown, Guyana, 27, 28 February, 1, 2 March
West Indies 352 (S.Chanderpaul 118, B.C.Lara 93) and 197
England 170 (M.R.Ramprakash 64 not out) and 137
Result: West Indies won by 242 runs.

Fifth Test
Kensington Oval, Bridgetown, Barbados, 12, 13, 14, 15, 16 March
England 403 (M.R.Ramprakash 154, G.P.Thorpe 103, C.L.Hooper 5 for 80)
and 233 for 3 dec (M.A.Atherton 64)
West Indies 262 (C.B.Lambert 55) and 112 for 2 (P.A.Wallace 61)
Result: Match drawn.

Sixth Test
Recreation Ground, St John's, Antigua, 21, 22, 23, 24, 25 March
England 127 and 321 (N.Hussain 106, G.P.Thorpe 84 not out, A.J.Stewart 79)
West Indies 500 for 7 dec (C.L.Hooper 108 not out, C.B.Lambert 104,
P.A.Wallace 92, B.C.Lara 89)
Result: West Indies won by an innings and 52 runs.

Angus Fraser's tour (all Tests):
Batting: 8 innings, 0 not out, high score 17, runs 44, average 5.50.
Bowling: 187.2 overs, 50 maidens, 492 runs, 27 wickets, average 18.22, best
8–53.